THE HOME BAR GUIDE TO

TROPICAL COCKTAILS

This book is dedicated to:
Kirby Fleming, Polly Fleming, and friends of the Rumpus Room.

Korero Press Ltd,
157 Mornington Road, London, E11 3DT, UK

www.koreropress.com

First published in 2019 © Korero Press Limited.

ISBN-13: 9780993337444

A CIP catalogue record for this book is available from the British Library

Editor: Suzy Lowey-prince

The tiki on the back cover was carved, in the Bumatay style, in 2018 by Scott Eskridge of Fallbrook, California and loaned to us for the photo shoot by our good pal Anders Anderson.

Printed in China

THE HOME BAR GUIDE TO

TROPICAL COCKTAILS

A SPIRITED JOURNEY THROUGH
SUBURBIA'S HIDDEN TIKI TEMPLES

KELLY "HIPHIPAHULA" REILLY
& "TRADER" TOM MORGAN

KORERO PRESS

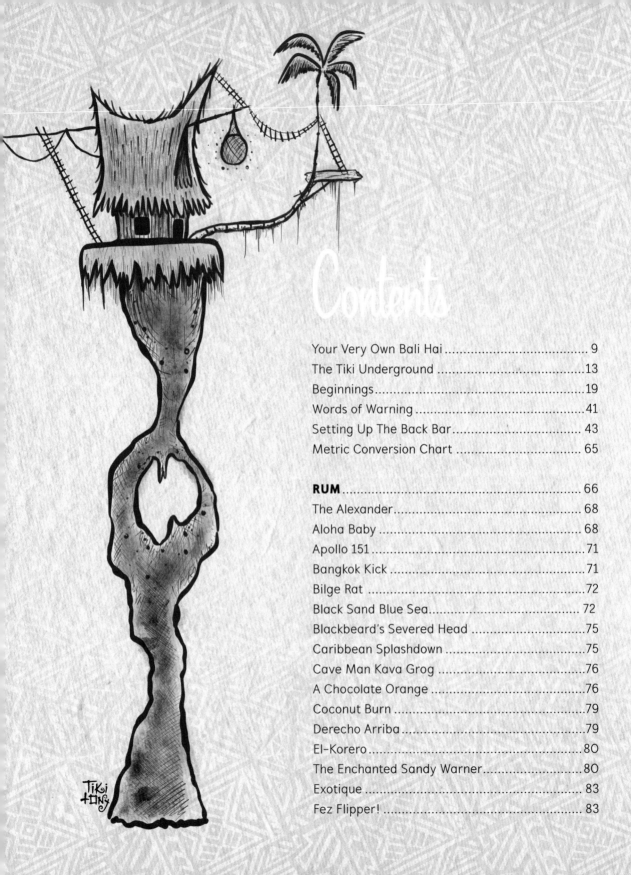

Contents

Tiki tony

APPENDICES

GLOSSARIES

INDEXES

Your Very Own Bali Hai

"YOUR OWN SPECIAL Island, Your Own Special Dream..."– This siren call from the musical and movie *South Pacific* rang true to many mid-century suburbanites in America. The desire to be a castaway on your very own Bali Hai became so strong that at some point it seemed that no self-respecting home, be it tract house or mansion, could be without its basement or backyard hideaway.

For certain individuals, the aesthetic trappings of the tiki bar tapped into archetypal desires. After being smitten on their first visit to such an urban island, be it a Beachcomber or a Trader establishment, they were infected by a tropical fever to become chief of their own "Quiet Village". Many who either couldn't, or had no desire to open fully-fledged restaurants, opted to create exotic Edens in the confines of their own homes.

Granted, not all dens, rec rooms, and family game rooms went tropical, and some barely reached beyond some fish netting, and cork floats to try to achieve the effect. But quite a few grew into floor-to-ceiling bamboo retreats complete with island murals and fake palm trees, astonishing neighbours and friends who then gladly gathered in these rumpus rooms for adult playtime.

Unfortunately, in recent years, many of these unique, personal visions of 1950s Polynesia Americana have been destroyed and torn out in the process of updating houses to whatever the current list of desirable materials dictated by the taste of the day has been. This process still repeats itself all over the United States.

Luckily, there has been a revived interest and appreciation in the rituals and customs of the post-war cocktail generation. The discovery of primitive artefacts and the unearthing of forgotten formulas of magic potions imbibed by the forefathers has inspired a new generation of tiki worshippers.

With the financial wherewithal of erecting a commercial tiki establishment being out of reach for most folks, many modern Polynesiacs have chosen to build their tropical oases at home. Aided by recent publications on the visual richness of mid-century tiki style, full-fledged tiki havens have sprouted up again in the basements and backyards of 21st Century America.

Kirby's Rumpus Room was such a place. Built with the artistic talent and ingenuity of its owner, it became the communal meeting place for the tiki-happy, sustained by their devotion for the pop culture, and their thirst for the rum rhapsodies served by Kelly Reilly (Hiphipahula) and Tom Morgan (Trader Tom).

Indeed, what would a tiki refuge be without its powerful liquid Voodoo to aid the paradise seeker in his quest for recreation. With soft Exotica tunes lilting in the background, tasty rum potions can send the land-locked sailor on a journey to exotic ports of call, where willing wahines sway in the warm climes of an eternal summer. The tropical cocktail has been the lifeblood of the tiki lounge, now and then.

Thanks to the tiki revival, true and tested tiki bar standards have been restored to their original taste glory, and many traditional recipes have been built upon and

Far left: Entrance to Ron and Mickee Ferrell's Rincon Room in Camarillo, California. Flanked by tikis, fishnets, nautical rope, and a warning sign about 'Dangerous Marine Animals Spotted In Area'.

Above: Interior of the Rincon Room in Camarillo, California.

Far right: Sven Kirsten built Silverlake Tiki Island in his Silverlake, California bungalow. It's filled to the brim with tiki items and predates the other home bars showcased in this book, having been built in the 1990s.

expanded to give tasty twists to old classics. To boot, a plethora of completely new concoctions have been created, craftily based on the concepts and formulas of original tiki mixology.

This collection of recipes is the result of the spirit of tiki tradition and innovation combined, a testament to the creative force of a unique concept of escapism that has lived on through the dedication and passion of those who regularly worship at suburbia's hidden tiki temples.

Sven Kirsten
Los Angeles

The Tiki Underground

THE TIKI UNDERGROUND is a casual social scene, rooted in no one particular place, where "tikiphiles" (fans of tiki) can hang out with like-minded friends and acquaintances. It's wherever people can feel free to argue tiki aesthetics and rum tasting notes with the fervour usually reserved for political debates. It's where a bottle of rum or a bag of limes is appreciated, but nobody is standing at the door to charge cover. It's where people appreciate classic tiki cocktails but also want to be introduced to something new: something that pushes the boundaries, but is still rooted in tiki history.

The Tiki Underground is one aspect of the Tiki Revival. Most tikiphiles have at least a passing knowledge of the rise and decline, and the eventual revival of tiki culture. Sven Kirsten has delineated this timeline in *The Book Of Tiki*. Kirsten goes into great depth, but in general terms, the timeline falls into the following categories: The pre-tiki period from the 17th to the mid 20th century, the golden age of tiki from the mid 1950s through to the 1960s, a tiki decline from the late 1960s through to the 1980s, and a tiki revival that appeared around the turn of the millennium but still endures to this very day.

Even a short internet search will show much evidence of that revival. There are now annual tiki events across the USA: from California, to Chicago, to Florida. Similar events have popped up in England, France and Australia. New tiki bars and restaurants still appear and are welcomed into the *Ohana* ("Family") each year. Otto Von Stroheim's magazine *Tiki News* paved the way for later events, publications, and clubs, like Tiki Oasis, *Tiki Magazine* and Poly Hai. Today, fans of tiki can indulge in a vast selection of art, carvings, and drinking vessels sold online or on location. All of these things are very public and easily accessible to those who are interested.

The flipside to that very public tiki revival consists of a deeply devoted core of hardcore tiki fans who organise semi-private get-togethers on a fairly regular basis through online forums, social media and word of mouth: *The Tiki Underground*. These hardcore fans do not think of Polynesian pop as merely a transitory experience. They might visit a previously unexplored tiki bar while on vacation, or drive great distances to take part in a weekend tiki event or host an annual summer luau for friends and family, but this is only the tip of the iceberg. Through great effort (and sometimes also great expense) they have created their own "Backyard Paradises," "Rumpus Rooms" or "Underground Basement Bars." For these die-hard tiki fans, tiki is something to be enjoyed all year round, 365 days a year. After all, if you've collected an impressive collection of tiki mugs, you want to display them. If you have a vinyl record collection, you want to play them. And, if you have rare rums that you've acquired, you want to savour them. But not just in the summertime. And not by yourself. That's no fun.

After immersing yourself in the pop Polynesian lifestyle, you want to share your experiences with other aficionados. But visiting a commercial tiki bar several times a week can be very draining for even the fattest wallets.

Far left: This depiction of the suburban Tiki Underground, beautifully painted by Doug Horne, shows a mid-century home guarded by a Bumatay-style tiki. The huge sign in the background is a playful nod to just how far some people go with their home bars.

Enter the home tiki bar. Now, the home bar is nothing new. However, its popularity in American culture has waxed and waned, often because of the economic climate.

The beginnings of home bar culture are rooted in the post-war era of the late 1940s through to the 1950s, which saw more people achieving their personal American Dream of owning their own homes. This allowed them more space to raise their families and, with that extra space, they had a chance to carve out adult areas for themselves. These "rumpus rooms" were the beginning. The overlap with the golden age of tiki (1950s-'60s) also explains why tiki was such a common theme in these home bars.

This post-war generation may have been more affluent than the one before, but they still had recollections of the Great Depression, and they understood the value of thrift (if they didn't, their parents reminded them). Even though they had the option of visiting a commercial tiki bar, it was often easier (and certainly cheaper) to invite friends over to their rumpus rooms and recreate the pop Polynesian experience in the comfort of their own homes.

There was also a do-it-yourself mentality that proclaimed it fun and challenging to use one's own talents to create a tropical home paradise, even if the results were not always what one hoped for. Episode 11 of the first season of *The Lucy Show* was entitled "Lucy Builds A Rumpus Room." In this episode, they try to convert their unused basement into a home bar and get stuck to the walls after applying heavy duty wallpaper glue. Other home bar builders from this period, however, had no problems at all. Folks from the neighbourhood would often chip in, and it was not uncommon for people's home bars to rival smaller commercial bars of the time.

People would even dress in a suit and tie to go to the neighbours: something that seems a bit unreal today. This formality extended into their leisure time in many ways. Later generations found this formality to be too stiff or "bourgeois" but those who appreciate vintage culture have a fond nostalgia for a time when people took pride in how they conducted themselves at home, instead of immediately changing into sweatpants once they've passed the home threshold — collapsing onto the couch to binge-watch whole seasons of a television show.

A sense of these older and elaborate home bars can be gleaned from the occasional estate sales of older homes where things have long gone untouched. Vintage photos fill in the gaps as well. And television shows from that era show just how ubiquitous the home bar truly was.

The heyday of home bars faded into the sixties and seventies. With the coming of the Vietnam War, a new generation rejected the social conventions of the ones before. People clamoured to go out and experience parties in larger group settings. The time and care needed to source cocktail ingredients and mix them properly fell by the wayside. Then came the prosperity of the eighties and the club scene went into high gear with hardly anybody considering home bars as anything but a dusty relic.

Things began to change in the late eighties and early nineties, though. Cocktail culture started making a comeback. Young people became interested in the leisure pursuits of their grandparents' generation. Many of the highly valued vintage pieces that now fetch top dollar were easily accessible to those willing to dig through the dust. And little by little, home bars started to make a comeback.

The economic climate also made this resurgence in home bar culture more appealing. As history shows, when times are tight, people stay close to home and pool their resources to have a shared communal experience. The Great Recession had a similar effect on the tiki community. There were already a number of fantastic home tiki bars in place when the recession began to hit in 2008. Many of them, however, saw only occasional use and were primarily spaces to showcase people's private collections and host the odd party.

Because of the economic downturn, this dynamic changed. Instead of using these tiki spaces infrequently for after-hours or small group invitations, many of these spaces started seeing monthly, or even weekly use. Additionally, the number of new home tiki bars being built saw a sharp increase.

This renaissance of home tiki bars was, as expected, very welcome. With some help from the tiki community and a willingness for several hosts to share the burden, a thriving tiki underground soon developed. Those in the know could travel every week or so and get their tiki "fix" for a fraction of what a typical night out on the town would cost. The commercial tiki establishments remained beloved fixtures, but the tiki underground became a nice supplement to indulge in on a regular basis.

Home bar tours (one of the earliest being the North West Tiki Bar Tour in Portland, Oregon) also began to thrive in other cities, including Los Angeles, and elsewhere. It is a major undertaking, however, to organise these events, and individual home get-togethers are more common.

Below: Dawn Frasier built the Bamboo Grove of Westwood, Seattle, Washington in 2008. Dawn is an accomplished artist who specialises in Mid-Century Modern-inspired tiki paintings, fabrics and textiles. She is probably best known for her *Moodxotica* paintings.

Tiki Central, a thriving online community of tiki enthusiasts, recognised this trend and in 2010 created a dedicated board to discussion threads that showcased home tiki bars. There had been disparate threads with pictures and discussion before this, but the interest in home tiki bars swelled to the extent that reorganisation was needed just to search and keep track of new postings.

Today, the *Tiki Central* forum on home tiki bars provides a valuable archive, and the threads range from minor enthusiasts looking to decorate a corner in their house, to professionally contracted showpieces with thousands of dollars spent and great attention paid to every minute detail. If you choose to go all out, there are tiki design professionals like Danny Gallardo (Tiki Diablo) who can be hired to transform your abode into a tiki oasis, and whose credits include such commercial tiki temples as The Golden Tiki in Las Vegas and The Tonga Hut in Palm Springs. Much of the most recent discussion and photos of home bars has migrated to other social media like Facebook. A great example of this is Adrian Eustaquio's Home Tiki Bar Builds Facebook Page. Humuhumu's well-known resource, critiki.com, now features home bars in addition to commercial tiki bars. Also of note is tikiwithray.com, Ray Wyland's tiki blog, which has dozens of home bar spotlights that go into great detail on the history and build-outs of home tiki bars. These websites and more each day offer a way for tiki enthusiasts to connect and share.

A great party can be had at any of these home bars with a little planning and help from friends. After all, it's not just art and architecture that creates the mood. With the proper music, a roomful of participants, and some delicious cocktails, you can turn the humblest tiki bar party into an event to remember.

So what is the future of the home tiki bar trend? Or of home bars in general?

In mainstream American Culture today, the idea of a themed room that people can escape to has been gendered into two main categories: "The Man Cave" or the "She Shed".

For today's men, the default is often to a sports bar/film theatre atmosphere. Some hearken back, however, to older models of masculine personal spaces and create library dens or trophy rooms with a Hemingway sort of vibe (African safari meets Cuban cigar lounge with a literary twist). Also popular are garage spaces where men showcase their love for cars, old tin signs, and nostalgic Route 66-style memorabilia. The show *American Pickers* is a prime example of catering to this niche market. There is a myriad of other themes, but these are a couple of the most popular. Tiki bars probably fall further down the popularity list as a mainstream favourite, but many bars incorporate tiki elements to achieve a generic tropical feel, even if they tilt more towards a Caribbean or Florida Key West look. It's not unusual to see tiki pulled in as a design element or to see Kustom Kulture, Rockabilly, or another sub-cultural ingredient mixed with more classic tiki. A love for vintage iconography, island escapism and rum cocktails blends nicely with many themes.

For women, the "She Shed" is often characterised as a lighter airier space that hovers uncertainly between a garden shed and a spa resort. It might have a crafting area, a place to quietly write, in, as Virginia Woolf might say, "*a room of one's own*", or it might merely be a place to lounge away from kids and family, with a hammock or day-bed. Tropical plantings and tiki-themed water features go a long way toward creating that exotic resort feeling.

While private sanctuaries have become more and more the focus, rather than spaces to entertain outside guests, this is not always the case. There are also elaborate

builds that include multiple rooms and adjoining backyards. These larger spaces are usually, though not always, made with an eye toward socialising and entertaining.

Entire television programmes have been devoted to exploring these niche design markets. The DIY (Do It Yourself) Network has a reality show called *Man Caves* that premiered in 2007 and is still presently on-air. Similar programmes are still being made each year, exploring the same topic. The Discovery Channel aired *Epic Man Cave Builds* in 2015.

Even within the tiki community, the allure of reality television has taken hold. Bamboo Ben (a professional designer for commercial and home tiki bars), Crazy Al Evans (one of the top modern-day tiki carvers), and Marina the Mermaid (an entertainer and professional mermaid) joined forces to create a pilot for their own tiki-centric reality show, tentatively titled *Building Paradise*.

It remains to be seen how much more into the mainstream home tiki bar culture will penetrate. Interest in it has ebbed and flowed over the years. However, as long as people seek a little bit of private paradise to hold onto, the option of a home tiki bar will be out there waiting for them. Moreover, by tapping into the community of tiki enthusiasts, these bars can also become part of the Tiki Underground, ensuring that the home pop Polynesian lifestyle stays strong for future generations.

Above: Tiki tOny's carving station. Among other items pictured are a vintage Harvey's bucket mug from Lake Tahoe, a souvenir tiki from French Polynesia, an old soup can with an umbrella that tOny joked was for making "Hobo Mai-Tais", and a hand-crafted mallet Tony uses for ice crushing, and citrus smashing.

Beginnings

I FIRST MET Kelly Reilly over the phone. It was 2006, and I was teaching a Public Speaking class at the local Community College. Her son, RJ, was one of my students. I had off-handedly talked of my fondness for collecting tiki mugs in class, and he thought it was a hoot that his professor shared the same weird interest as his mother.

When RJ told her, Kelly could not believe it. She had been collecting for years and wanted to chat. So she called my number off his student syllabus, and we talked for a good hour about all things tiki-related.

Later, we met up at a local tiki event and soon became fast friends. At first, we talked mostly about mugs, but over the next couple of years, our interests branched out into other tiki pursuits as well. Especially cocktails. I had a fully stocked home bar leftover from my bachelor days. It had been gathering dust for a few years, but I dusted it off and began focusing exclusively on tiki drinks.

It was a heck of a lot of fun: much more challenging than the drinks my friends had requested back in my twenties.

Kelly, unbeknownst to me, had also been experimenting at home. We compared notes and decided it would be fun to team up and pool our liquor cabinets together.

Fast forward three years to 2009, and something happened to kick our cocktail experiments into high gear...

A mutual tiki friend, Kirby Fleming, opened up his newly built home bar, The Rumpus Room, to guests.

He graciously allowed Kelly and I to put our skills to the test behind his bar. And we took advantage of it, almost every week, for the next couple of years.

It was a welcome release for me. I was deep in the trenches of finishing up a PhD, and it gave me a chance to focus on something entirely different. There was a sense of camaraderie and adventure. We were happy to take requests but more and more frequently, Kelly, and I would use the time in the Rumpus Room as a learning laboratory, and we'd get instant feedback on what succeeded and what didn't.

We began spending all our extra cash on rare rums and liqueurs, exotic fruits from our local Asian markets, and making rum infusions and homemade syrups. Each week we'd try to work on something different, and everybody that attended would kick in something as well. Sometimes it was simply some citrus to be juiced. Other times it was a bottle of rum to replace what we were running short on. Most memorably, I remember our friend Anders Anderson (A-Frame) coming in with a one-litre jug of Dagger Rum that he'd scored from the clearance shelves of a mom and pop liqueur store. Dagger was once the go-to rum for many of the Mai-Kai's cocktails down in Florida (and many other bars as well). It was legendary.

Not every day was a success. Some days only one or two people would show up. Or a much-anticipated ingredient would turn out to be a dud. I think the Durian fruit extract from a small Asian grocer in San Gabriel was probably my worst purchase. If nothing else, if this warning can save somebody from what might best be described

Far left: Kirby Fleming built the Rumpus Room in La Crescenta, California in one half of a two-car garage during 2008-2009. The house was inherited and had been in his wife's family for 60 years. The back portion of the garage had been used as a laundry room and as a "Rumpus Room" before that. With the help of friends, it took about three months to complete. Kirby is best known for his artwork and tiki carvings.

as a "garlic custard fruit" that eclipses any other flavour, then the writing of this book will have been worth it.

We also had the occasional argument. I started out believing that price was no object in the quest for a good cocktail. Kelly knew this wasn't always true and admonished me to use combinations of cheaper ingredients instead of always reaching for the top shelf — challenging me to be more frugal. Sometimes a splurge is called for, but we developed a sliding scale, learning to use whatever we had behind the bar to make the tastiest cocktails possible.

It wasn't like learning on the job at a commercial bar. It was more unpredictable at times, and usually a bit more laid back. Some evenings, there would be less than a dozen people, and we could take our time and do jigger pouring and experimentation. Other nights, though, it would get very busy. We had nights with fifty or more people, and we'd have to scramble to make drinks and keep ingredients stocked.

Eventually, we fell into a rhythm with some people bringing certain ingredients. Volunteers arrived early to do the juicing. Some people brought in snacks from local bakeries or other LA eateries.

It's only in retrospect that I appreciate what a golden era our time in the Rumpus Room was. Since those early days, I moved to Portland with my family for four years and then moved back to Los Angeles. Much has changed. Kelly has set off on her own;

Below: The Wrecked Wench in Winnetka, California was built by Jake Geiger in 2012, and is a mixture of pirate and tiki theme. Jake is a graphic artist for the gaming and entertainment industries, and his house showcases his own art as well as those elements he finds inspirational.

as an independent bartender, she has helped with private parties all over Southern California and worked at celebrated bars like The Tonga Hut and La Descarga.

Commercial bars and tiki events seem to be thriving all across the country, but the spirit of home tiki bartending continues. Numerous home bars have sprung up to carry the banner, including the Desert Oasis Room, the Waikiki Womb, the Wrecked Wench Bar, the Flaming Tikis' Bar, and the Lothario Lounge to name a few.

Kelly and I have worked behind many of these home bars, concocting drinks with whatever dusty bottles we might find... supplementing with some of our own stock that we lug around behind us... and it's always a good time. Evenings go by so fast we barely have time try to jot down notes to remember what worked and what didn't.

This book is a much prettier version of that rum-stained Rolodex of recipes that we've collected over the years.

We hope that you enjoy trying these drinks and that you feel inspired to experiment with your home bars, to host more parties, and add a new chapter of your own to the history of home tiki bartending.

"Trader" Tom Morgan

Above: The Tiki Hut in Yucaipa, California was built in 2012, with the help of family and friends, by Erich Troudt. It took three and a half years from start to finish. The hut houses a collection of mugs, Coco Joe's, Witco pieces, matchbooks, tourist souvenirs, nautical artefacts and several tikis, including a 7-foot-tall Maori carving from Jungle and Sea Imports, and an 8-foot-tall Papua New Guinea statue shown above.

The Rincon Room in Camarillo, California was built by Ron and Mickee Ferrell in 2005 and took ten months to complete. It was one of the earliest and most elaborate builds in the new wave of home tiki bars. Ron sells lamps, mugs, and other creations under the Rincon Trading Post brand.

The Lili Kai Club in Commerce Township, Michigan was built by Jeff Bannow and completed over about a year from 2016 to 2017. As Jeff explains, "The name mashes together *lilikoi* (passion fruit) with *kai* (ocean), and club (a large piece of wood used to hit people over the head)."

The Black Lagoon Room in Cudahy, Wisconsin was built by Pete Klockau and Katie Monachos in about six months during 2017. It is a basement bar located within a 1953 mid-century modern Frank Lloyd Wright-acolyte designed split level house on the shores of Lake Michigan.

The Beachcomber Shack in Ventura, California was built by Tiki tOny in 2011. It serves as a hangout and a workshop. Tiki tOny is known for his tiki carvings and artwork.

The Desert Oasis Room in Corona, California was built by Adrian "Polynesian Pop" Eustaquio in 2010 and took about four months to build. Adrian is best known for his podcast, *Inside The Desert Oasis Room*.

Ken's Tiki Lounge in Lomita, California was built in 2004 by Ken and Gloria Hudson, in a converted garage in the couple's home. They are avid collectors of Polynesian art and artefacts and are especially proud of the many pieces recovered from now-defunct tiki establishments.

Matt "Spike" Marble built the Breezeway in Costa Mesa, California in 2012. It took about a month to complete but with a lot of help from friends, including Bamboo Ben. Matt is best known for his band, The Hula Girls.

The Overlook Lounge in Fresno, California was built by Mark Skipper, a classic car enthusiast and tiki aficionado, in 2016–2017. In addition to being a spectacular home bar, it has been used for several tiki-themed pinup shoots.

The Waikiki Womb in Glendale, California was built by Kevin (Murph) and Claudia Murphy in 2007 and closed in 2014 when they sold their home and relocated. Kevin and Claudia are both partners in running the well-known commercial tiki bar, The Tonga Hut.

Caroline Roe & Robert Fertig built the Moai Icehouse in Austin, Texas in 2017 with some help from Bamboo Ben. Caroline is a founding member of the Fraternal Order of Moai and the organiser of the Ohana Luau at the Lake and Texas Tiki Week in Austin.

Trader Dick's in East Brookfield, Massachusetts was built by Richard Barnes in 2015. It had started out as a mixed theme hunting lounge and man cave, but after a trip to Trader Sam's at the Disneyland Resort, it was soon converted to a full-on tiki theme.

HaleKahiki, Michael Uhlenkott and Alan Smart's home bar in Echo Park, California was built over four months in 2006. "HaleKahiki" translates roughly to "Tahitian Home". Alan is known for his work as an animation director. Michael is an artist, musician, and surfer.

Side view of the HaleKahiki, Michael Uhlenkott and Alan Smart's home bar in Echo Park, California.

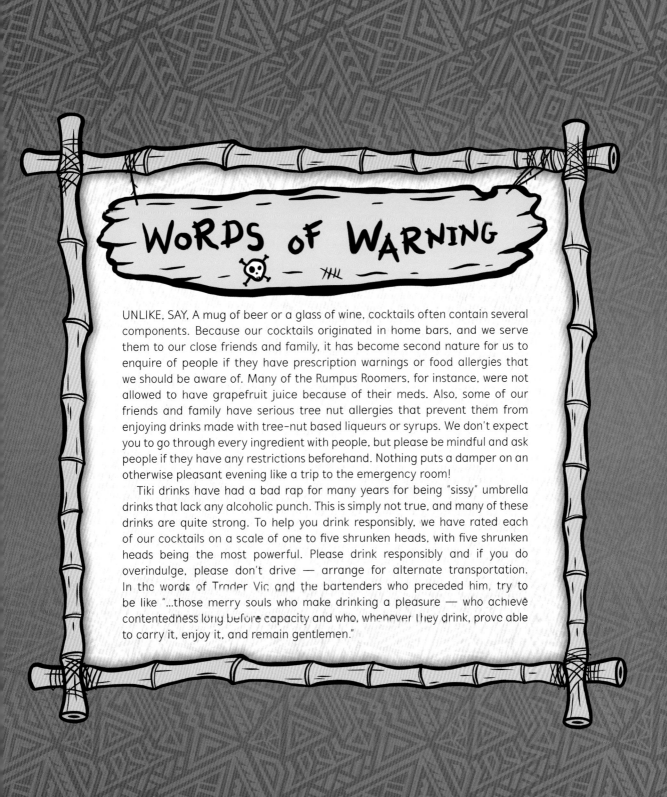

WORDS OF WARNING

UNLIKE, SAY, A mug of beer or a glass of wine, cocktails often contain several components. Because our cocktails originated in home bars, and we serve them to our close friends and family, it has become second nature for us to enquire of people if they have prescription warnings or food allergies that we should be aware of. Many of the Rumpus Roomers, for instance, were not allowed to have grapefruit juice because of their meds. Also, some of our friends and family have serious tree nut allergies that prevent them from enjoying drinks made with tree-nut based liqueurs or syrups. We don't expect you to go through every ingredient with people, but please be mindful and ask people if they have any restrictions beforehand. Nothing puts a damper on an otherwise pleasant evening like a trip to the emergency room!

Tiki drinks have had a bad rap for many years for being "sissy" umbrella drinks that lack any alcoholic punch. This is simply not true, and many of these drinks are quite strong. To help you drink responsibly, we have rated each of our cocktails on a scale of one to five shrunken heads, with five shrunken heads being the most powerful. Please drink responsibly and if you do overindulge, please don't drive — arrange for alternate transportation. In the words of Trader Vic and the bartenders who preceded him, try to be like "...those merry souls who make drinking a pleasure — who achieve contentedness long before capacity and who, whenever they drink, prove able to carry it, enjoy it, and remain gentlemen."

Setting Up The Back Bar

KELLY IS THE one who usually sets up the back bar area so fastidiously when we bartend together. But since I'm the long-winded one, you'll have to put up with a little of my philosophising as well.

This topic reminds me of a summer weekend morning many years ago when I lived in Pasadena, California. At the time, I was teaching night classes and working on my dissertation. I seldom rose before 11 a.m., but on this day, my wife woke me up with the phone in her hand, urging me to take the call. I figured it must be something really serious and braced myself to hear of an accident or death in the family.

It was neither.

On the other end was a friend from our regular Rumpus Room get-togethers. He told me there was an estate sale just blocks from my house and that the backyard and double garage were decorated in old school tiki décor. He also warned me that the word was out, and I wasn't likely to pick up much when I got there, but I decided to make the attempt nonetheless.

I jumped out of bed, threw on some clothes, and hurried over.

Once there, I saw several smiling people from the tikiphile community that I recognised, many of them carrying big boxes of vintage tapa lights and mugs over to the estate liquidator.

I hurried past them and entered a two car garage that must have been someone's tiki lair since the early 1950s. It was in rough shape and mostly gutted, but I could see the bones were there as my eyes slowly adjusted to the dark interior...

A belt-driven fan system with tropical fronds no longer worked and electrical cords hung lifelessly from the ceiling where lamps had been removed. The far corner had a bamboo fountain with a broken pump. One whole wall was covered with hundreds of large abalone shells whose iridescent insides caught the light. I thought of salvaging them, but on inspection, each was nailed to the wall by rusted carpentry nails with no hopes of removing them short of sawing out that section of the garage. A milk crate caught my eye. It was filled with Hawaiian themed vinyl records. The lp covers, though, had mildewing around the corners and I have horrible allergies to mould and mildew. No thanks! The far corner had a built-in bamboo bar that had seen better days and all alcohol had been removed long ago...

It looked like a bust.

I decided to search without being so dependent on my eyes to guide me. I stood behind the bar to gain my bearings and reached behind some bamboo trim, in the same basic area where time after time I, myself, had tucked away important information while busily making drinks. I came away with a cocktail booklet from the early '60s and several cocktail recipes that had been cut out of Hawaiian newspapers and magazines. Muscle memory had served where the eyes had failed me.

Likewise, I meandered over to a maintenance area in back of the garage, where dusty tool cabinets and cans of paint sat silently, totally ignored by the tiki hunters.

Above: Orchids of Hawaii bartender's guide and catalogue, 1981.

Far left: The back bar of The Moai Icehouse in Austin, Texas which was built by Caroline Roe & Robert Fertig in 2017 with some help from Bamboo Ben (interior designer for many commercial and residential tiki bars). The bar top is made up of shards of broken tiki mugs as well as other tiki ephemera, all sealed under a coat of clear resin.

Above: This is an Edgar Leeteg tribute piece entitled *Cheers to the Hina Rapa* by Doug Horne. Leeteg's work has influenced many of today's current tiki artists.

I felt along a shelf that lay in the shadows. Right where I would have put something if I wanted it out of sight...

That's where I found a rolled up paper that, once unfurled, proved to be a 1960s menu cover from Chi Chi's in Las Vegas. This tiki restaurant had blatantly ripped off Edgar Leeteg's popular velvet painting of a half-naked wahine ("Hina Rapa"), and the home bar owner had ripped them off in turn. It had probably hung proudly in his tiki bar until some prudish relative had wandered in and torn it down from its place of honour.

Again, logical guesswork based on the layout and my muscle memory of having placed things just out of sight in my own garage.

I proudly carried my paper finds up to the estate liquidator who shrugged and charged me only $5 for the paper ephemera, dismissing them as worthless compared to the bigger items others had carried away. But to me, they were priceless.

I suppose I could be glib at this point and say that I used the "Tiki Force" or some such thing to find these objects. The truth is much more interesting, though.

When I was a young teen I spent a couple of consecutive summers with my grandparents. I learned a great deal by observing my grandfather who had been a school teacher his entire life. In his 60s, however, he lost most of his eyesight, and could only see the vaguest of shadows when something moved.

His entire house was set up logically and neatly so that he could retain his independence and find anything he needed when he needed it. Logic and muscle memory allowed him to live fairly normally.

In fact, he took up new hobbies! He learned to paint. Mostly landscapes. By plotting out the geometry of the horizon lines on the canvas, he was able to envision country roads, train tracks, rolling hills, and distant mountains.

He also taught me several boy scout knots, chastising me when I failed to follow his slow and patient lead. How could I complain to him that it was too hard?

From him, I learned that sight is a valuable thing, but by being methodical and constantly practising, one can manage without it.

Just as the fastest typists don't need to look down at the keyboard, you can step up your speed and serve drinks much faster by carefully planning out your back bar environment. And, as he would say, "No excuses!"

Behind The Bar

Much has been written and discussed about decorating your home bar and creating the proper lighting and ambience, but let's stop and think about where hardly anybody ever looks...

Kelly and I agree that this is the one area in your tiki space that needs to operate as close to a commercial bar as possible to make it run smoothly and make your parties a success. But if you've never worked in a bar, how will you know this?

How should you arrange it to make your bartending as easy as possible?

How do you fix it so that, eventually, you can let muscle memory take over even with your eyes closed?

Although many home bars are stuffed with collections, densely layered, and darkly lit, I've found that those that have been around for a while tend to gravitate toward the same sort of easily navigable back bar arrangement.

THESE 5 PRINCIPLES OF TIKI BACK BAR ARRANGEMENT ARE AS FOLLOWS:

- **Have room to breathe.** Before you start to get too invested in stocking your new space, make sure you can squat down and easily turn 360°. Ideally, you want to have four feet of space behind you as well. Otherwise, you will find yourself becoming claustrophobic and will probably end up breaking some valuable bottles. That six-foot tiki, should not be behind the bar. It will serve you better in its own space, where it can shine in its own glory. De-clutter as much as possible.

- **Make commonly used items more accessible** with an eye towards economy of motion so that grabbing ingredients becomes muscle memory and not a scavenger hunt. Nothing slows you down more than over-stuffed canisters holding tools, some of which you may never use (even if they were a wedding present). Keep it simple with a jigger, a metal shaker, a bar spoon, a flat bottle opener, a muddler, a strainer, a knife and a pen. Other tools can go in a drawer under the bar.

- **Forego the need to display everything** and hide backup supplies in cabinets out of sight. Glassware or extra alcohol bottles may look impressive all lined up like soldiers preparing for battle, but eventually they will need to be dusted or washed. Worse yet, they crowd your working space or tempt others to use them in lieu of already open bottles or the primary glassware you intended to use. Also avoid displaying all your tiki trinkets in this space. Show off that Coco Joe and coconut monkey collection elsewhere, as you will need every inch of space you can find.

- **Have a house specialities emphasis**, and don't prepare or stock for everything at once. Trying to buy everything will hurt your pocketbook. Also, by concentrating on a smaller menu of drinks, you will become more expert in those drinks before moving onward. Lastly, your guests will want to bring gifts and it's tough to shop for the person who has everything. If there's something you are interested in mixing with, mention it to others and they may get it for you. Don't buy it immediately. Exercise impulse control.

- **Lastly, have enough lighting** to mix but still maintain ambience. I know I just talked at length about being able to do things while blind, but that doesn't mean you HAVE to! Sometimes someone might move something that you had carefully arranged. Also, swag lamps are beautiful, but it's sometimes hard to make out labels in that kind of softly lit environment. The 151 and the 80 proof rums might get confused and it could be quite a surprise to your patiently waiting guest! To this end, you might consider a light under or adjacent to your bar. Not a flashlight as those tend to disappear faster than a loaned out ballpoint pen. A clamp light will work. A pendant light or two with a tight focus can also come in handy. You might also have a tikified desk lamp or cocktail table lamp from your favourite tiki palace of long ago.

Additionally, here are some specific components and observations on what does or doesn't work for stocking your home tiki bar:

WHAT ALCOHOL TO STOCK?

The recipes in this volume reflect our experiences at a number of very different home bars. Some of them were very elaborate and stocked all the best rum and alcohol that money could buy, rivalling some commercial bars. Other home bars were very modest and were lucky to have one or two common bottles of rum available.

You can have wonderful experiences at either type of bar with a little planning and forethought. Buy within your means and purchase rums and other alcohol that you personally enjoy mixing drinks with. That way, if it is not all consumed, you are not stuck with a dusty bottle that will never be used. Check out our appendices in the back of this book for guidance. Never be afraid to reach out to your community if you need added supplies. Guests seldom arrive empty-handed, and if you let them know what needs to be re-stocked ahead of time, they will happily chip in with precisely what is required. I am often reminded of the old folk story about stone soup in which each guest brings a small ingredient that culminates in a savoury soup for everyone to enjoy. Same principal, only better, because we're talking cocktails here!

As you read these recipes, you will see that some of them are a bit vague, calling for "dark rum" and some of them may be very specific, calling for a brand like Coruba Dark or Appleton Estate 12 Year Old Rare Blend. This is simply because some recipes were invented using specific alcohols and some were recorded after having been field tested with several varieties with a great degree of success using different varieties of rum to personal taste.

You should feel free to adapt and replace specific rums and alcohols in these recipes to fit your preference and budget. Each recipe is a treasure map, but whether you get there by bicycle, Lamborghini, or army tank, is up to you.

BACK SHELVES

This is usually where the alcohol is kept. Some people keep their best spirits on the traditional top back shelf which is at eye level for guests and makes a nice display but be aware that they will focus on the most interesting and expensive spirits and ASK for them. I know! The audacity! So only display what you are willing to open and mix with. Otherwise, it's just a tease. Worse yet, somebody who doesn't appreciate the top shelf ingredients will ask for it just because it is there. Nothing is worse than politely pouring someone a shot or two of expensive alcohol that they turn away from after barely a sip because it's "not to their taste." Such a waste. If it is out of sight and someone still asks for it, chances are they will appreciate it much more! Every bartender has a different philosophy. As a rule, Tom likes to pour, but Kelly hoards.

SPEED RAIL

This is a smaller shelf, usually kept close at hand. It will hold the most often-used spirits. If you have a huge liquor selection, this will save you time and energy, making the night go much more smoothly. I usually have six to eight bottles that I draw from frequently over the course of an evening. If they were mixed in with a 100 other bottles of alcohol, it would make it much harder to pour as quickly.

When laying out the plan for your bar space, whether you are building it from scratch or using a freestanding bar, try to use the "lip of the bar" so that you can bolt on two-speed rails or a double shelf rail. If you only have room to install them behind you, try to put them somewhat to the left or right, so they are not directly behind you. Kelly still has flashbacks to time spent in one particular home bar where the speed rail was installed directly behind her in a cramped space, and she had to do so much awkward twisting that it made it more a nuisance than a convenience. You can purchase speed rails from most restaurant supply stores, but you will find a wider and cheaper selection online. You're sure to find a style to suit your bar's needs.

Far left: A collection of several spirits and flavoured liqueurs other than rum. Many of these flavourings can be attained at home by infusing plain spirits or simple syrups. For instance, the Ancho Reyes is made with ancho peppers and we have an ancho syrup recipe on page 238. The saffron-infused gin could be infused at home using your own gin and saffron to taste. There are many recipes for pimento allspice dram, and we offer a syrup version on page 241. Do not feel limited to what is on your liquor store shelf. There is always a solution.

BITTERS

Since these are like salt and pepper for your cocktails, used in small increments for a finishing touch, they are usually kept close at hand to the side of the main bar area. Drink makers have recently upped the amount of bitters in their cocktails compared to traditional drinks. However much you are using, they are used frequently and so need to be closer than some of the lesser used spirits and liquors. Angostura in the large bottle used to be the standard choice, but now there are countless designer flavours from celery to rhubarb. Here are just a few brand options:

- Angostura
- Bitterman's
- Bob's Bitters
- Fee Brothers
- Peychaud's

...or you could make your own

GLASSWARE & GLASSWARE PLACEMENT

Vintage glassware was smaller. This made sense because smaller servings meant that you were enjoying a crafted drink that would stay cold. Much of today's glassware is oversized because many people feel that "bigger is better" and they are getting more value if their cocktail is bigger. Big glasses are harder to keep cold, and you tend to end up with a watered-down drink, or, if you imbibe it too quickly, you end up over-serving yourself. With the craft cocktail movement, however, people have become less concerned with quantity than quality, and now glassware is reflecting a return to the smaller versions of yesteryear.

You can purchase full sets of well made and standardised glassware new. Cocktail Kingdom is a good source. However, if you would like to have it personalised for your home bar, you can do that as well. South Pacific Promotions has been one of the leading glassware suppliers to the tiki community since 2004 and can make your designs a reality.

Typically, I would advise people to first have an ample supply of both highball glasses (sometimes people use standard pint glasses or a 12–16 oz glass for a highball glass) and a good supply of lowball glasses (also called Rocks glasses or Old Fashioned Glasses) on hand. You may also want to stock some tiki mugs or tiki bowls. As you move forward, you can purchase martini glasses, shot glasses, coupes, snifters, and other glassware should the need arise. You can either find vintage drinkware or buy new pieces directly from such suppliers as Tiki Farm and Munktiki. Most people in the tiki community have collections of rare pieces they have collected. I don't recommend drinking from something that you would shed real tears over if it slipped from your hand during a party.

Keeping glassware in a spot that is unlikely to gather dust is always a good idea. I prefer to keep them in closed cabinets close at hand to the bar (or inside it) if possible. However, at the Rumpus Room and other home bars, guests often bring their own favourite tiki mug or glass that is easily identifiable and not likely to get mixed up with others as they mingle throughout the evening. Some even bring their own reusable straws. Not only does this spare you wear and tear on your own glassware and mugs but if they have their own, they will likely make sure that they are clean for next time, sparing you some washing up.

Whatever you do, don't use plastic, especially red solo cups, if you can help it. You won't be struck by a lightning bolt out of the sky, but it's a major downer to go to a carefully curated tiki party that creates a wonderful ambience except for the ubiquitous red cup. If you absolutely must use plastic for budgetary reasons or high-volume parties, try to use 100% clear plastic. Choose 10-12 oz plastic glassware as a standard. Any larger than this and you will probably end up having a higher ice to less liquid ratio. As our natural instinct is to fill a glass with ice, you could run short. Plus, it's a poor presentation to have so much more ice than liquid in a cup.

ICE, ICE CRUSHER & SCOOP

Crushed ice is crucial to most tiki drinks. If the ice is too fine, it turns the drink into a slushy. If the ice is too coarse, it doesn't have as much surface area to melt and blend with the other components. Crushed ice aerates a cocktail to enhance the blossom of the spirits and leaves a beautiful natural froth on top after mixing. Big cubes melt much more slowly. This is why punch bowls are always cooled using block ice. Crushed ice in tropical cocktails is calibrated to dilute the cocktail in precisely the right way, and it has a pleasant mouthfeel. If you forego the straw, you can sip down a few small slivers of ice with your drink to keep it chilled as it goes down.

Achieving crushed ice can be accomplished in several different ways:

- Just buy a bag of it already crushed. Often, grocery stores will use a bed of crushed ice to lay out their seafood for display and if you sweet-talk them, you can buy some clean crushed ice for personal use. Or, you may find another source if you do some careful sleuthing around at your local ice house, ice cream truck service, or party supply store.
- Old fashioned hand crank machine. These come in two sections with a metal hand crank. They've been around for years and are fine if you are going to make just a few drinks by grinding up larger cubes.
- Built-in refrigerator ice crusher. I have one of these, and you can fill individual glasses from the door of the refrigerator (until you go through all the reserve ice which is usually four or five trays worth).
- A stand-alone electric ice crusher. There are some excellent machines out there that can be bought used or new. I've used several, and they vary, but if I were to recommend a new one, it would probably be the Waring Pro IC70 ice crusher.
- A mallet, a canvas Lewis Bag, and cubed ice can produce crushed ice for a few drinks. It's impressive to hammer your ice for a drink or two, but if you have to make 50 cocktails, this method would quickly get old.

A blender, however, can't crush ice properly. Either you go too far and have a slushie, or not far enough and end up with larger chunks of cracked (not crushed) ice.

Sometimes, if I am making a lot of cocktails, I prefer to mix crushed ice with larger cubes and thus spread out the effect somewhat. It's a halfway measure that can help you to make crushed ice last longer.

Ice is always one of the things that you run out of at parties. No surprise then that ice, along with limes, is one of the most commonly requested things for guests to bring. And, if you run short of either one, that basically ends your bartending for the evening until more can be found.

If this section seems like too much obsessing over ice, consider what our ancestors had to go through. Read Henry David Thoreau's *Walden* and its section on the ice-cutters in the chapter "The Pond in Winter", where the thick layer of ice covering the pond was laboriously broken up and carted away for sale in town. Or rent the film *The Mosquito Coast*, starring Harrison Ford and River Phoenix, where they risk everything to bring ice to the natives. All things considered, we have it relatively easy today!

I suggest getting a metal scoop to shovel ice out of bags or buckets. Some people improvise with red solo cups or other items, but these get broken or lost. Metal scoops also help to break up ice when it melts and fuses together into larger chunks. I've picked up a few of these over the years, usually from restaurant supply stores. One note on scoops: do not put them through your dishwasher as they will oxidise and darken. Handwash them to keep them silver and new-looking.

Make sure your ice is as fresh as possible and hasn't picked up refrigerator odours and gone stale. Nothing is worse than making a delightful drink and ruining it with disgusting ice. I usually keep a couple of Baking Soda boxes in my freezer just to be safe, but you should always sample the ice beforehand if you have any doubt.

Lastly, you will find that some cocktails (although the recipe calls for crushed ice) just can't be shaken with crushed ice. For a professional appearance, you often must strain the cocktail to a glass filled with crushed ice.

REFRIGERATOR
A small college-sized mini fridge is probably good enough. If you have space, however, you can go as large as you want.

COMMON MIXES TO KEEP REFRIGERATED
- Coca-Cola (Mexican Coke with cane sugar preferred)
- Ginger Beer (not ginger ale)
- Seltzer or Soda Water (not tonic water with quinine)
- Pineapple Juice
- Orange Juice
- Guava Nectar
- Coconut Cream
- Homemade Syrups should be kept refrigerated to maintain their shelf life. Be sure to label and date them so you can keep track of how long they last and if they are still good.

PRE-SQUEEZED OR FRESHLY SQUEEZED LEMON AND LIME JUICE
"Nothing tastes better than freshly squeezed juice!" is an understatement. The next best thing is pre-squeezed lime or lemon juice which often comes in large containers and can only be found at wholesale supply houses. If you own a business and have the proper licences, you can purchase from these, or if you know somebody who does, this will save you hours of work, especially when it comes to batch mixing for a huge party.

Lime juice tends to go faster as it is more often called for in tiki cocktails. It is a good idea to prep the juice before a home tiki bar event. Most juice tends to do well for several hours after being squeezed. After that, it will start to oxidise and not taste as fresh. Some people freeze their leftover juice for later.

In a pinch, if you run out of juice, there are alternatives from your liquor store or grocer. There are some decent brands of sour mix starting to come out on the market. Beware, because most of them are still caught in a chemical haze leftover from the 1980s. Avoid the cheapest chemical-laden products. Additionally, there are small grocery shelf bottles of freshly squeezed key lime juice available as well. Key limes have a slightly different flavour but can work well in many cocktails or when mixed with regular lime juice.

Refrigerating Coco Reàl makes it almost too thick to squeeze out of its plastic bottle. Better to leave it at room temperature if you want to use it often and don't plan on having it sit around for months at a time unused. Coconut milk is canned so it probably needs to be transferred to an airtight container if you have some remaining after use. It is more likely to need refrigeration once opened if you don't plan on using it right away. Both products will stay fresher longer if refrigerated after opening.

JUICER (HAND, ELECTRIC, OR STANDING)

For any of these juicers, make sure that you also have a sharp knife and cutting board to accompany them. If you are making just a few cocktails, then a hand squeezer will suffice. The enamelled green ones are everywhere, but there are more industrial and long-lasting naked aluminium ones available. For large gatherings, you will want to have something a bit heavier duty. Electric juicers work well enough, but many of them jam, need frequent cleaning or, in the worst case, burn out their motor. Kelly recommends the Black & Decker 32 oz Citrus Juicer CJ630. It is a surprisingly inexpensive juicer. Although it's loud and clumsy, she has never burnt out one of these machines, and while she might have been forced to buy more than one because she misplaced earlier models, their motors have lasted through thousands of hours of juicing. Rather than invest in another electric juicer (after I burned out a couple of non-Black & Decker versions), I eventually went with an industrial table-top lever press model. This is the kind frequently used by people who are pressing tons of citrus for canning/preserves. They can be found at industrial restaurant supply stores. I like the cantilever action, the simplicity of the design, and the fact that it is easily cleaned and may well last past my lifetime. Granted, it is big, expensive and takes up space, but you can't have everything.

BAR TOOLS AND OTHER ESSENTIALS

There are a lot of expensive sets out there, but you can also put together a very functional and affordable set of vintage or used tools sourced from thrift stores or garage sales. If you want to purchase new tools, Cocktail Kingdom's online catalogue gives a wonderful selection. Or, you can shop on eBay to find the perfect vintage set to match your bar. Be careful not to let style outweigh substance. You want something that is comfortable to use, easy to clean, and that will last for many years to come.

- Cobbler Shaker (three-part metal) or Boston Shaker (pint glass and metal top)
- Jigger
- Long Bartender's Spoon
- Hawthorne Strainer
- Peeler
- Pineapple Corer
- Knife
- Cutting Board
- Muddler
- Lemon Extract
- Sugar Cubes/Croutons
- Cinnamon Shaker
- Eye Dropper
- Lemon and Lime Juice Squeeze Bottles

Kelly prefers the Boston Shaker because it is easier to separate when it ices up. The Cobbler Shaker can sometimes be hard to separate. Try to get a heavier gauge stainless steel shaker and not one of the lighter gauge shakers handed out for alcohol promotions.

As for jiggers, I don't recommend a cheap one. Look for one with precise measurements that fits comfortably in your hand and which you can flip back and forth to use either side easily. These have a larger measurement on one side than the other and can be found in ½ oz / ¾ oz, 1 oz / 1½ oz, and 1 oz / 2 oz. Jigger pouring is the hallmark of making tiki-style cocktails and the bane of many high volume commercial bartenders who are used to "free pouring" by timing the length of the pour for an approximate amount. Tiki cocktails are all about precision. In fact, you will note some of our recipes call for .33 oz (or ⅓ oz) which would require estimating a third of an ounce sized jigger. Because they often taper from top to bottom, this is sometimes difficult. But with patience and practice, you will get the hang of it.

Kelly reminds me that you can buy some very accurate stainless steel jiggers at restaurant supply stores and because they are held accountable to larger corporate buyers, the measures are correct. When I think of cheap jiggers, I think of the ones that come in cheaply produced home bar gift packs and almost always end up thrown away or in a bargain bin at the thrift store. In any case, please shop around for the best and most accurate you can find. Kelly recommends Kegworks online for jiggers and other barware and tools.

There are some lovely vintage long bartender spoons, but, again, for a new one, I would suggest checking out Cocktail Kingdom's selection online.

Hawthorne strainers come in almost every set of bartending tools. If you buy a vintage one, make sure the coiled spring is still firmly attached.

Peelers can be found at most groceries and kitchen supply places. OXO brand has a nice range of products.

Don't use too big a knife. Find a paring knife that fits comfortably in your hand.

The cutting board should be small, easy to clean, and preferably machine washable. Ideally, store in an upright position.

Don't spend your life savings on a muddler. There are some extravagant versions out there.

Lemon extract has alcohol in it, but more importantly, it has essential lemon oils that create a much more impressive flame when you light a flaming garnish on top of a drink than overproof rum You will need a wick to absorb this extract, and most people use a sugar cube or bread crouton to achieve this. Most of our recipes mention using overproof rum for flaming garnish, but lemon extract produces a superior flame.

Sugar cubes are handy if you need to add sugar but are out of sugar syrup, and it's easy to muddle them to powder, and they will then dissolve easily. I also prefer to use a sugar cube or a VERY light unflavoured bread crouton as the wick for flaming drinks. Set it within a hollowed-out lime shell and douse it with a little lemon extract. The croutons can smell a bit off-putting at times but this is usually clouded by the lemon smell, and if you add cinnamon for flame/spark effects, it adds a pleasant aroma as well. If you are doing a flaming garnish, be thoughtful about placement, as you don't want to melt plastic straws or set fire to drink umbrellas.

The cinnamon shaker is useful with flaming drinks to give a gust of fire and showmanship. You can buy an inexpensive metal shaker at most kitchen supply stores. Or, control your dosage with a pinch of cinnamon in your hand. Please practice your technique ahead of time as some people use too much and end up setting their thatched tiki bar roofs on fire. I have seen it happen at even the most respected tiki bars. BE CAREFUL!

Eye droppers are useful when measuring minute quantities of powerfully flavoured liqueurs like Pernod or Absinthe.

The juice squeeze bottles should be clear and easily cleanable. Buy the quart-sized bottles as you will use more juice than you anticipated. You can label them with a colour-coded decal/sticker or colour-coded caps. When in doubt, use the sniff test.

TOP-DOWN MIXERS AND BLENDERS

Sometimes referred to as a single spindle or "flash blender". Don the Beachcomber started a craze for 151 Swizzle cocktails that he made in a top-down mixer and served in metal swizzle cups. To this day, top-down mixers are popular among tiki cocktail enthusiasts, especially those made by Hamilton Beach because they stir ingredients well without turning them into a slushie. Blenders are usually used to "flash blend" for no more than 5 seconds or so on high, lest the drink turns into a slushie. If you really want to homogenise ingredients for, say, a piña colada, then a blender will be useful on your bar top. Otherwise, you can probably get away with just the top-down mixer for the most part. Top-down mixers, it should be noted, are easier on your shoulders than shaking tins vigorously all night long. Many bartenders with a solid top-down mixer end up doing much less shaking. If done correctly, there is no dilution of the drink, and you can go faster with less effort.

FLOOR MATS AND TOP BAR MATS

You can buy plain black ones through wholesale restaurant supply stores, or you can hunt around for ones imprinted with your favourite brand of spirits. You will want a solid rubber floor mat to prevent slipping behind the bar where it gets slick. Also, the floor mat provides some cushion during extended periods of standing and pouring drinks. Good shoes are a must as well, but a floor mat is equally important.

PAPER TOWELS AND BAR TOWELS

I always keep a roll of paper towels at hand in addition to the traditional cotton bar towel. Lots of spills will happen and depending on your set-up, you may not always have time to wring out a cotton towel and rinse it out. Paper towels are a fast fix sometimes.

SINK/BUCKET

Ideally, in a commercial establishment, you would have a three-sink set-up, but most home bars are lucky if they have one small bar sink. In a pinch, a five-gallon bucket will serve to dump unwanted drinks. You can collect and dump out the bucket at the end of your party and then wash it along with your other glassware.

GARNISH CADDY

Typically, you will want to have tropical garnishes, including pineapple chunks, maraschino cherries, orange wheels, and mint sprigs. As part of the show, you should display these prominently around the top of the bar and finish off your drinks with style. Garnishes such as mint also have a pleasant aroma and add to the overall experience. You may have glass dishware to hold these items, or you may want to purchase compartmentalised garnish caddys, with covers, to preserve the freshness of your ingredients. With mint, it is also a good idea to wrap the cut ends loosely with damp paper towels to retain freshness, so they don't wilt. For display purposes,

you may want to keep the wrappings out of sight, but before and after serving, you can re-wrap them. Again, commercial style caddies can be purchased at wholesale restaurant supply stores.

NAPKIN AND STRAW CADDY

These are a must to better (and more quickly) serve your friends and protect your bar top and other furniture. Find your favourite brand online.

CARVED GARNISHES

One of the most popular garnishes these days, popularised by Chicago's Paul McGee and his staff (first at Three Dots and a Dash and later at Lost Lake), is the banana dolphin. Whether it's a banana dolphin or a piece of lime peel carved into a skull shape, or some other invention, these carved garnishes push your presentation up a notch and make the drink that much more enjoyable. Many garnishes are inspired by the fruit and vegetable carving that is popular in Thailand. There are entire books on vegetable carving available. Let your imagination soar and create some themed creations for your own house menu.

PICKS/STRAWS/UMBRELLAS/SWIZZLES

Royer is the commercial swizzle maker for most tiki bars. If you want to go so far as to have your in-house swizzle sticks, they would be happy to work with you. Royer has a minimum order, though, so unless you are prepared to have them for a lifetime, think twice before investing. Other items, such as straws, umbrellas, and picks can be ordered cheaply through wholesalers. Smart & Final or Party City have many of these supplies. You might also try Cost Plus World Market.

BOTTLED WATER (NOT FOR MIXING)

With the emphasis on cocktails, it is easy to overlook the need to supply bottled water, or a water dispenser of some sort. Designated drivers can't be expected to sit quietly throughout the evening with no beverage to sip on. If someone does accidentally imbibe too much, they will want water to help clear their system and stay hydrated since alcohol can dehydrate one leading to terrible hangover headaches.

BOTTLE POURERS (SPEED POURS)

Kelly and I often dispense with regular bottle tops (keeping them in a spare drawer in case we want them later, especially if travelling with or if shipping opened bottles) because they tend to become crusty with sugary evaporated liqueurs and are often hard to remove. Instead, there are lots of quality pour spouts (speed pours) available through restaurant supply stores or online. Kelly prefers speed pours on all bottles except those spirits which are seldom used, and with those, she will leave on the manufacturer's cap and pour from the bottle to a jigger. Also available at the restaurant supply stores are rubber nipples that cover the speed pours, which are a convenient must. Choose speed pours with screens in them because it's so easy to attract barflies in even the cleanest environments (insert bar joke here). Kelly will never use the ball bearing speed pours because they are slow and become clogged and break.

COCKTAIL BOOKS AND COCKTAIL NOTES

Most home bars will have a small stack (or even a full shelf) of cocktail books to refer to. In our modern age, smartphones give us access to quite a bit of information, but books allow us a more tangible and personal reading experience. Plus, the anachronism of everyone dressing in aloha shirts and drinking in an immersive tiki environment is somehow destroyed and undercut if everyone is hunched over and involved with their smartphones. To preserve your books and keep them from getting sticky, you should have them on a nearby shelf or in a cabinet away from possible spills. Also, if you have room, you might want to get a cookbook splatter screen that keeps your book open but protects it from squirting citrus and spilt cocktails. Kelly recommends copying and laminating pages from your favourite books and thus keeping your original books from getting damaged.

TIP JARS OR NO TIP JARS?

This is really a personal decision, depending on the type of party you are throwing. If you are throwing parties very rarely and want to provide everything out of your own pocket, without expecting anything in return, then that is fantastic. However, if you are throwing regular parties, the recurring expenses will add up, and guests are more than happy to pitch in to make sure that the strain doesn't become too burdensome. Guests can contribute in different ways. Some may contribute labour by helping to squeeze citrus juice beforehand. Some may contribute food or snacks. Some may contribute bar supplies that are regularly needed (or some speciality alcohol that you may want, but not necessarily for the party). Some may be happy to put cash in your tip jar. The bottom line is that you should not be afraid to ask for help or contributions if you feel you need to. No one should expect you to provide an unending free party place.

Additional Concerns

CLEANLINESS AND BARFLIES

Barflies are usually used as a colourful term for regulars at dive bars. The term, however, refers to real insects as well. We tend to forget this, as our society now has health inspectors and most people are much more careful than in previous generations. Their official designation is Drosophila melanogaster, and these little annoyances are attracted to sugary and wet substances. They have a 48-hour lifespan, so if they occur, you can get rid of them in 2-3 days tops with some vigorous cleaning and airing out of your bar. If you clean your bottle tops, speed pours, spill mats, floor, and trash can, there shouldn't ever be a problem.

TEMPERATURE AND SPIRITS

I'll never forget the afternoon I spent pouring hundreds of bottles of wine (mostly) and spirits down the kitchen drain. They had arrived at my house the week before from a family friend who left them to me as part of his estate after he died. This guy had lived off the grid in Arizona, and the contents of his house had sat in that desert heat for who knows how many years before I came into my inheritance. A college friend toughed out the sampling with me. If a bottle passed the visual test and smell test, we took a tiny sip. Not many passed. I think at the end of the day we came away

with a nice bottle of Bénédictine and three bottles of whiskey. Wine is much more temperamental, but most spirits should be stored at temperatures that you, yourself, are comfortable living at. If you have an un-air-conditioned tiki hut in the desert, you should plan ahead to move your booze for the hot summer months. If you wouldn't leave a family pet in those temperatures, don't leave your alcohol there either.

IN CASE YOUR ALCOHOL COLLECTION EXCEEDS YOUR SPACE

This is a common problem. In the same way that tiki mug collections expand beyond their limits, you may acquire or be gifted with more alcohol than you can comfortably store or display in its designated area. One more obvious way to deal with this is to buy more shelves or another piece of furniture. If you are in a tight space, however, and have already used up your wall space, this may not be an option.

An alternative solution is to invest in a bar cart. Some people depend solely on bar carts to store bar supplies. For overflow, however, it is a great solution, because if it is in the way, you can wheel it into another corner or out of the room. It can also serve as a make-shift speed rail if wheeled up alongside your main bar area. You can stock it with most of the things you want to use immediately, and when the party is over, you can clear it away when you have time.

I have a vintage rattan cart with glass shelves that I picked up from a Craigslist ad fairly cheaply. It blends in nicely with the rest of my tiki room. There are a host of styles ranging from sleek and modern to faux antique versions with ornate carved wood details and gilded decorations. If you pick out a rugged model, you might even be able to use it both indoors and out. This would let you move the party indoors in case of rain or back out again to take advantage of great weather.

GROWING YOUR OWN INGREDIENTS

- Mint
- Lemons and Limes
- White Grapefruit vs Ruby Reds
- Oranges
- Blood Oranges

In Southern California, if you don't have a citrus tree in your yard, the chances that somebody in your neighbourhood does. Between harvesting local citrus and gardening a small supply of mint or other herbs, you can stock your bar shelf nicely. This short list offers just a few examples plus some general observations to keep in mind wherever you happen to live.

Mint grows like wildfire. Be careful not to plant it in a borderless flowerbed, or it will take over. I grow mine in a half-barrel planter and keep it in a shaded area with plenty of water. If tended, you should rarely run out. When keeping picked mint in the refrigerator, you can wrap it loosely in damp paper towels to preserve its freshness longer.

There are varieties of lemon that can taste quite different. With their distinct flavour profile, Meyer lemons are a favourite of bartenders. Make sure you check to see which type of lemon your recipe calls for.

Generally, I tend to encounter two kinds of limes — small Mexican limes or larger limes of the Bears variety in California that are called Tahiti or Persian in some places. I avoid the Mexican limes because they have less juice and I'm usually in a hurry. One

Far left: Trader Tom's rattan bar cart being put to good use at Tiki tOny's Beachcomber Shack.

The Overlook Lounge in Fresno, California was built by Mark Skipper, a classic car enthusiast and tiki aficionado, in 2016-2017. In addition to being a spectacular home bar, it has been used for several tiki-themed pinup shoots. This photo shows a nautical influenced area within the Overlook Lounge that has a model ship, topless hula girl masthead, diving helmet, and shelves of taboo vintage tiki mugs safely tucked away behind the bar.

way to extract more juice is to roll the limes on a cutting board before slicing. My lever press juicer, however, hardly leaves a drop of moisture, so I've become lazier with that method of late. Lime juice is used more often in tiki cocktails than lemon juice, so if you are stocking up, make sure you err on the side of more limes.

White grapefruit is beloved by tiki cocktail enthusiasts for many drinks, such as the popular Navy Grog. White grapefruit, however, is being phased out by growers in favour of the sweeter and more easily grown Ruby Red variety. White grapefruit can be found during a very short season, so plan those drinks accordingly. Substituting Ruby Red will throw off your drink recipes and using bottled white grapefruit is a sad substitute for fresh.

The evils of prepackaged orange juice are well known. Because of its homogenous nature, however, you can be sure of consistency when using it. Freshly squeezed orange juice can vary wildly, and although it can be delicious, it sometimes happens that you will get some not so tasty oranges in the mix. Always be sure to taste what you've squeezed before you mix it into an expensive cocktail.

Blood oranges can be amazing both in colour and taste. The flavour has been embraced recently across a wide spectrum with blood orange liqueurs, syrups, and sodas. The environment of the tree, the amount of water, and the temperature can have a huge effect on the fruit, however. Again, always be sure to taste what you've squeezed before you mix it into an expensive cocktail.

THE TIKI UNDERGROUND HOME BAR PARTY TIPS

Home tiki bars are often eclectically outfitted and you will run into a unique range of concerns that would probably never come up in a commercial bar.

Some of this information you've doubtless come across when other sources discuss luau parties, but recurring events have their own unique share of concerns. If you plan on hosting several such events, be aware that your initial parties will set up a set of ground rules and expectations that are hard to course-correct if you don't make them clear early on.

The following list overlaps concerns for those who are self-hosting and those who are organising/bartending a party at another person's home.

TABOO TERRITORY

Parking is the very first concern, and if it's not handled correctly, it can put a damper on any future events. Make sure you alert your guests as to the best way to handle parking once they arrive.

Seating and flow-through for guests should be anticipated beforehand. It makes everything so much easier. Interrupting things to run and find chairs or move furniture around, once you start mixing or playing host is best avoided.

Some house areas are going to be off limits and for a variety of reasons. Maybe there are messy bedrooms you don't want to be seen. Maybe you have valuables or work materials you don't want to be disturbed. Usually keeping things dark or locked up does the trick. If you inform some of the first guests they can usually pass the information on for you and keep an eye out for other guests who arrive later.

As a showcase area, home bar owners probably have objets d'art that they would lose their mind over were they to be broken, stolen, or even touched. Often, these objects are right beside objects bartenders will need to use. So, make sure to re-arrange or mitigate the chances of something happening before a party if possible.

Likewise, not all spirits are meant for the sampling. If a host has a few bottles of rum that are off limits, make sure that whoever is bartending does not dip into their special stash. Either remove them to another area or cover the tops with upside down plastic cups or flag them as off-limits in some other way.

WHO IS GOING TO BARTEND?

Sometimes a host wants to bartend, but hosts should not be bartenders all night because it prevents hosting, especially if there is a large and demanding crowd of drinkers. If a host wants to make the occasional drink or two, that is understandable, but somebody needs to step up to provide relief when necessary.

Bartenders can sometimes delegate on occasion and make people feel useful and included (cutting lemons and limes, squeezing juice, or taking out the trash). However, you don't want everyone to think it is a free for all. If everyone goes behind the bar, then things get messy or lost, making it harder for the bar to function.

Some home bars are very tiny and only allow one person to be behind them at a time. So, if you were planning on having two people back there, you might have to change your plans based on the home bar in question.

Some successful home bar parties plan ahead and give shifts to different bartenders so that maybe each hour or so has a new bartender with a signature drink or two at hand. Some parties have a main bartender and one or two guests who have an understanding that they may be called to bat when necessary throughout the evening.

However you arrange it, try to plan ahead as much as possible, but keep it fun at the same time. Nobody likes a grumpy bartender or party planner. With some thoughtfulness and willingness to go with the flow, everyone should have a good time and not feel overly burdened throughout the party.

GETTING READY

Party punches can take the pressure off a bartender and decrease the amount of jigger pouring. Usually, these are cooled by a big block of ice that melts more slowly than crushed or cubed.

Paper Towels, garbage containers, and other basic supplies should be well-stocked beforehand.

Ice, pre-squeezed juice, and other basic supplies should be checked and double-checked.

Provide bottled water and snacks for those not drinking and to provide some respite from the rum.

Delegating responsibility and being considerate will go a long way toward making the evening successful. Some people step up to help with certain chores, but they should never be given too much to do or go unrecognised for their efforts. Burnout can occur in even the most exuberant volunteers. Likewise, not every exuberant volunteer can do all tasks. Be careful who you delegate to.

In addition to a punch bowl, you might consider a clear dispenser. Kelly and Tom both make use of clear plastic 3½-gallon drink dispensers. We usually mix all of our ingredients in a plastic 5-gallon Igloo dispenser so that it can all be stirred together well without sloshing out the top. We then fill the 3½-gallon dispenser to the top just before the party and place the Igloo cooler out of the way until we see the level has gone down far enough that a refill is in order. Don't forget to provide ice and cups. Having these drink dispensers constantly flowing can take a burden off of the bartenders so they can comfortably mix drinks at a large party without having a frustratingly long line.

DRINK WARE

"Glasses or tiki mugs?" is a question that often gets asked. Many hosts that serve tiki cocktails are also mug enthusiasts, but by putting your drink in a mug, you don't showcase the look of the cocktail. Guests may see the garnish, and that's about it. So, if you want to profile the look of the drink, glassware is often necessary.

That said, many guests at regular get-togethers like to have their own personal mug to use, and if they want to be responsible for keeping it clean and washing it out in the sink and putting it back on a shelf for you, then it cuts down on the clean-up you have to do.

What to use depends on how many are attending, your drink list, and how much you care about spending time on clean-up. Plan ahead, however, and you will thank yourself later.

RESPONSIBILITIES OF GUESTS AND HOSTS

Hosts need to give guests some expectation of what they are supposed to contribute to a tiki party ahead of time. This not only expedites things but prevents hurt feelings and misunderstandings. Some things will be decided on the fly in a more organic way, but the more that you can plan ahead, the less stress you will have and the more smoothly things will go.

- Tips
- Supplies
- Labour
- Clean-up

GIVE THE BARTENDER A BREAK

Bathroom and off-the-feet breaks are necessary for everyone, and your bartender will perform better with frequent breaks. In addition, as said earlier, hosts should not be bartenders all night as it prevents hosting.

The bar needs to remain a sacred space. If you're a guest, don't go behind it if you haven't been invited and don't help yourself to supplies, even ice without asking. In front of the bar, you should enjoy yourself as a guest, but be considerate of the bartender and other guests. Don't monopolise the bartender with speciality drink requests or long conversations that make it hard for them to help the other guests.

LAWSUITS AREN'T TIKI AND CAR ACCIDENTS AREN'T EITHER

Accidents happen, especially when booze is involved. As a non-commercial establishment, you may not be prepared to deal with litigious guests. A gopher hole in the yard or piece of broken glass can spell the end for any future get-togethers.

Just as you would baby-proof a house before new parents bring over their toddler, you should drunk-proof your home to prevent accidents as much as possible.

As the saying goes, an ounce of prevention is worth a pound of cure. Keep plenty of bottled water and soft drinks at hand as an alcohol alternative.

Keep a careful eye on guests and if someone is too inebriated or unsteady on their feet, try to help them out or enlist other guests to assist you. Likewise, be careful not to over-serve guests who might turn into drunk drivers. Ride shares between guests or a taxi can save the evening and many future evenings to come.

**ALOHA AND FAREWELL. 'TIL WE MEET AGAIN.
(AND YOU'LL GET LIMES AGAIN NEXT TIME, RIGHT?)**

Too many times it's easy to be caught up in the moment and then suddenly the party is over, and half your guests are leaving. Social media is great to follow up with but be sure to touch base with people before they go if possible.

Be sure to thank those that did pitch in and to make all the necessary farewells that are expected of a good host.

Some guests will silently slip off like ninjas but do your best. Not everyone wants or needs a long goodbye, but try to be as aware and considerate as possible as the night comes to a close.

Don't just concentrate on serving the die-hards hanging out to the bitter end or on cleaning up the mess immediately. If it doesn't get done that night, you can get it the next morning. Just be practical and clean up anything sticky, so it doesn't attract bugs.

If anything is needed for the next party, now is often a good time to confirm with guests who will be bringing what.

Above all, remember to enjoy yourself and encourage pictures (especially group ones) to share with friends and encourage future events!

Metric Conversion Chart

Alas, there is no single units of measures in use around the world. Even ounces and pints are different between the UK and the US. We made this simple conversion table to help you. A good bartender should always use relative measures in their recipes. One and a half ounces is typically called a shot.

cup	oz* ounces (US)	tbsp tablespoon	tsp teaspoon	ml milliliters
1	8	16	48	240
3/4	6	12	36	180
2/3	5	11	32	160
1/2	4	8	24	120
1/3	3	5	16	80
1/4	2	4	12	60
1/8	1	2	6	30
1/16	1/2	1	3	15
1/32	¼	½	1 ½	7.4
1/64	⅛	¼	¾	3.7

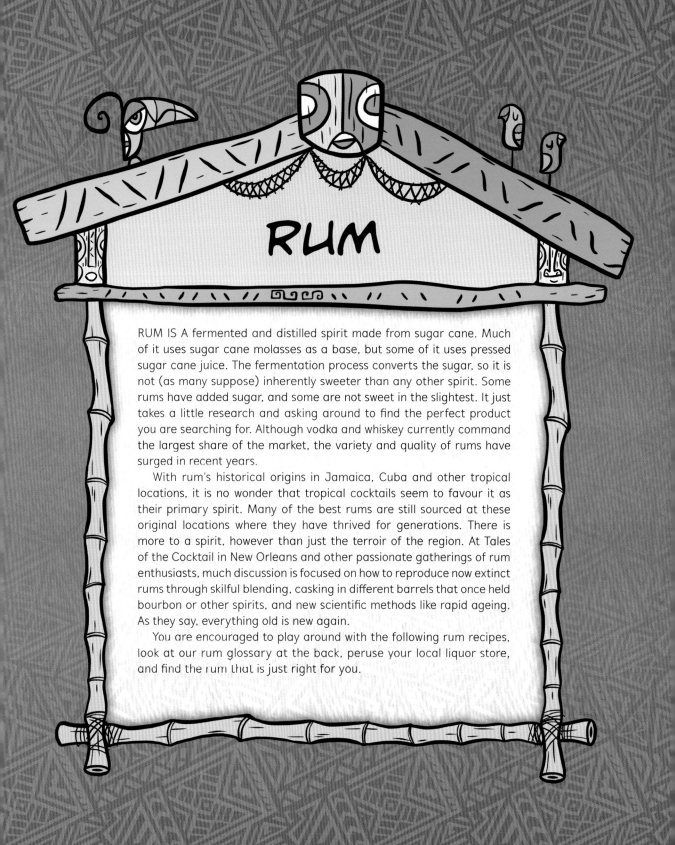

RUM

RUM IS A fermented and distilled spirit made from sugar cane. Much of it uses sugar cane molasses as a base, but some of it uses pressed sugar cane juice. The fermentation process converts the sugar, so it is not (as many suppose) inherently sweeter than any other spirit. Some rums have added sugar, and some are not sweet in the slightest. It just takes a little research and asking around to find the perfect product you are searching for. Although vodka and whiskey currently command the largest share of the market, the variety and quality of rums have surged in recent years.

With rum's historical origins in Jamaica, Cuba and other tropical locations, it is no wonder that tropical cocktails seem to favour it as their primary spirit. Many of the best rums are still sourced at these original locations where they have thrived for generations. There is more to a spirit, however than just the terroir of the region. At Tales of the Cocktail in New Orleans and other passionate gatherings of rum enthusiasts, much discussion is focused on how to reproduce now extinct rums through skilful blending, casking in different barrels that once held bourbon or other spirits, and new scientific methods like rapid ageing. As they say, everything old is new again.

You are encouraged to play around with the following rum recipes, look at our rum glossary at the back, peruse your local liquor store, and find the rum that is just right for you.

The Alexander

One of Kelly's creations. No relation whatsoever to the Brandy Alexander. Kelly's The Alexander is inspired by the "Alexanders" of Palm Springs, California. The Alexander Construction Company built over 2,200 houses, in the modernist style between, 1955 and 1965. The Alexander cocktail was designed for the 2012 Palm Springs Caliente event where the Rumpus Room hosted a room party of their own. Palm Springs is also known for its date palms and with this recipe's delicious date puree you can have a spicy and intoxicating date night whenever you want!

2 oz Coruba or Cruzan Coconut Rum

1 tbsp Homemade Date Puree

¼ oz Orgeat Almond Syrup

¼ oz Pimento Allspice Liqueur

½ oz Freshly Squeezed Lime Juice

½ oz float of Appleton 12 Year Jamaican Rum

¼ oz Cruzan Blackstrap Rum

TO SERVE
Add all the ingredients into a shaker tin with crushed ice and shake vigorously. Strain all ingredients into a chilled saucer or large champagne coupe and add ice. Float the Appleton 12 Year Jamaican Rum and garnish with a fresh flower.

STRENGTH SCALE

Aloha Baby

A Kelly recipe inspired by the Tikiyaki Orchestra song and album of the same name. Created at Kirby & Polly's Rumpus Room in La Crescenta, California. Try this unique island style cocktail, topped off with a float of Dark Jamaican Rum. You want even more coconut? Add some coconut cream. Tall and refreshing. Aloha, Baby!

2 oz Coconut Rum

¾ oz St. Germain Liqueur

1½ oz Homemade Hibiscus Syrup

¼ oz Orgeat Syrup

1 oz Kern's Farm Guava Nectar

½ oz Torani Passionfruit Syrup

1 oz White Grapefruit Juice

1½ oz Freshly Squeezed Lime Juice

1 oz Freshly Squeezed Lemon Juice

1 oz float of Dark Rum

TO SERVE
Shake with crushed ice. Serve in a hurricane glass with a pineapple wedge on the rim and a flower garnish.

STRENGTH SCALE

Aloha Baby

The Bangkok Kick

Apollo 151

A Kelly cocktail that will make you BLAST OFF! With Lemon Hart 151 Rum, Martinique Rum, and a lingering whisper of nut and vanilla liqueurs, it will leave you breathless.

1 oz 151 Lemon Hart or Hamilton 151 Rum

¼ oz Clement V.S.O.P. Martinique Rum

1 oz Orange Juice

1 oz Tuaca Liqueur

⅛ oz Orgeat Syrup

¼ oz Simple Syrup (optional, in lieu of sugar swizzle)

2 drops Absinthe

TO SERVE

In a rocks glass filled to the top with crushed ice, add all ingredients, then transfer all to a shaker tin and shake. Pour back into the rocks glass. Garnish with a very light dusting of nutmeg, sugar swizzle across the glass, and an orange peel floating on top.

STRENGTH SCALE

Bangkok Kick

Tom and Kelly invented this in 2009, during a mixology test kitchen night. If you like Thai flavours, prepare yourself for a spicy treat!

2 oz Homemade Ancho Chili Pepper Syrup

3 oz Plantation 3 Star Light Rum

1 tbsp Peanut Butter (or substitute 1 oz Castries Peanut Liqueur)

½ oz Freshly Squeezed Lime Juice

1 oz Coconut Cream or Coco Reàl

TO SERVE

Pour into a pilsner glass and garnish with a couple of raw sugar cane swizzle sticks and a lime and a cherry on a spear.

Honestly, if you use peanut butter, it often takes work to dissolve into the drink, although it may surprise you if it's really warm and smooth. Using a peanut liqueur is easier, or you can make peanut orgeat as discussed in the appendices.

STRENGTH SCALE

Bilge Rat

Created for Jake Geiger's Home bar, The Wrecked Wench, in Winnetka, California. Come aboard and join Kelly's crew if it's a kegger of rum yer dyin' to partake of, matey. Liquid gold with four kinds of rum and many a citrus, so you don't get the scurvy now — if the rum don't kill ya first. Aye!

1 oz Coruba Dark Jamaican Rum

1 oz Sailor Jerry Spiced Rum

1 oz Mount Gay Eclipse Barbados Rum

½ oz Disaronno Amaretto Liqueur

¼ oz Homemade Pimento Allspice Dram Syrup

½ oz Christian Brothers Brandy

1½ tbsp Brown Cane Sugar (dark)

1½ oz Orange Juice

1½ oz Blood Orange Syrup (Torani)

1 oz Freshly Squeezed Lime Juice

1 oz Freshly Squeezed Lemon Juice

Float a dash of Cruzan Blackstrap Rum on top

TO SERVE

In a shaker tin add all the citrus juices and dark brown sugar, stir and set aside. In another shaker tin add crushed ice and the remainder of all the ingredients. Next, combine the brown sugar and juices in the tin with the rums and liqueurs and flash blend or shake vigourously. Pour into a rum barrel mug or pirate drinking vessel.

STRENGTH SCALE

Black Sand Blue Sea

Kelly took it as a challenge to create a better blue-coloured cocktail. This drink was made for the Tikiyaki Orchestra in 2010. When Kelly first heard the Tikiyaki Orchestra's song "Black Sand, Blue Sea" it took her away to a place she wanted to be and to stay forever, lying on the sand sipping her ultimate island style cocktail. This drink is guaranteed to also take you where you want to be.

2 oz Cruzan Coconut Rum

¾ oz Blue Curaçao Liqueur

1 oz Coco Reàl Squeeze

1¼ oz Freshly Squeezed Lime Juice

Flash blend, then float:

5 dashes of Pimento Allspice Syrup

⅓ oz Cruzan Blackstrap Rum

¼ oz Crème de Cassis

⅛ oz Caramel Syrup (optional)

TO SERVE

In a tin blend Cruzan Coconut Rum, Blue Curaçao, Coco Reàl, and Freshly Squeezed Lime Juice, then flash blend for about 5 seconds. Pour into a piña colada glass (smaller hurricane-style glass) and float Pimento Allspice Syrup, Cruzan Blackstrap Rum, Crème de Cassis. For a dessert version, add some caramel syrup. Garnish with a pineapple chunk and a cherry speared through with a paper umbrella. The finished drink looks good with its layers, but one should stir this cocktail with straw or swizzle stick before drinking.

STRENGTH SCALE

Black Sand Blue Sea

Blackbeard's Severed Head

Blackbeard's Severed Head

Both Tom and Kelly made this cocktail. Careful not to drink too many or you might lose your head!

3 oz Kraken Spiced Rum

2 oz Appleton 12 Year Rum

1 oz Ancho Reyes Liqueur

1 oz St. Elizabeth's Allspice Dram

2 oz Torani's Passionfruit Syrup

2 oz Freshly Squeezed Lemon Juice

2 oz Freshly Squeezed Lime Juice

A big splash of Club Soda Water

TO SERVE
Build in a shaker tin with crushed ice and shake vigorously, then pour into a Blackbeard's Head mug and add ice to the top. Serve with a float of Mount Gay Eclipse Black Overproof Rum and fill the spent lime shell with part of that float. Then light on fire. Sprinkle some cinnamon from a shaker to create a shower of sparks in memory of the firecrackers that Blackbeard wore in his beard to frighten his enemies.

STRENGTH SCALE

Caribbean Splashdown

Did you know the majority of U.S. Mercury and Apollo space capsules splashed down in the Caribbean? You do now. Kelly has carefully blended this cocktail to make sure your evening splashes down in just the right spot!

1 oz Plantation 3 Star White Rum

1 oz Brinley Gold Shipwreck Vanilla Rum

½ oz Blue Curaçao

¼ oz Galliano Liqueur

1 oz Freshly Squeezed Lemon Juice

⅛ oz Cinnamon Syrup

TO SERVE
Build the cocktail in a collins glass of crushed ice, shake vigorously or flash blend, then transfer back to the Collins glass. Garnish with a dust of cinnamon. On an umbrella, place a cherry, a piece of pineapple and a lime wedge and hang on the rim of the glass.

STRENGTH SCALE

Cave Man Kava Grog

Kelly consulted with several physical anthropologists on this one. It's the missing link you need to get in touch with your primal self. Back in the Stone Age, this concoction of Pusser's Navy and Coruba Dark Rums was only for the keepers of the cave. Today the Caveman Gods let you take part.

1 oz Coruba Dark Jamaican Rum

1 oz Pusser's Navy Rum

½ oz Triple Sec Orange Liqueur

1 oz Freshly Squeezed Lemon Juice

1 oz Dole Pineapple Juice

½ oz Torani Passionfruit Syrup

½ oz St Germain Elderflower Liqueur

A dash of Velvet Falernum

A dash of cinnamon on top

TO SERVE
Serve in a pilsner or pint glass or your favourite tiki mug. Garnish with a sprig of mint and a chunk of pineapple and a cherry on a spear.

STRENGTH SCALE

A Chocolate Orange

Kelly invented this in 2009. A nod and a wink to the film director Stanley Kubrick for the name, but the flavour is pure English Christmas orange — the chocolate kind you smash before unwrapping to eat "slice" by "slice." There is a similar product sold by the bottle called Sabra liqueur. It's a chocolate-orange flavoured liqueur produced in Israel, but the Godiva/Cointreau version above is a bit mellower, and you can make a little at a time, so you don't overindulge your sweet tooth.

¾ oz Godiva Chocolate Liqueur

¾ oz Cointreau Liqueur

TO SERVE
Shake with crushed ice and then strain and pour into a lowball or double shot glass for quick and easy. Or for a more polished look, serve in a small snifter with a sugared rim and an orange wedge for garnish.

STRENGTH SCALE

Cave Man Kava Grog

Coconut Burn

Coconut Burn

This cocktail was invented during a travelling Rumpus Room at Kevin and Claudia Murphy's Waikiki Womb Home Bar in Glendale, California, by both Tom and Kelly. Light, sweet, and with some heat. A fan favourite.

1½ oz Coconut Rum (Cruzan preferred)

½ oz Homemade Ancho Chili Pepper Syrup

1 oz Seltzer Water

½ oz Freshly Squeezed Lime Juice

5 oz Crushed Ice

TO SERVE
Flash blend for 4 seconds with a top-down mixer. Serve in a highball glass with a paper umbrella stabbed through a lime wedge on the side of the rim.

STRENGTH SCALE

Derecho Arriba

Tom invented this drink at the 2015 Wrecked Wench Halloween Party in Winnetka, California. The word *derecho* comes from Spanish for "straight," and describes a long-lasting and severe squall line with strong straight-line winds. Must be at least 50 knots to qualify as a derecho. Comparable to a hurricane which clocks in at around 64 knots or more. Sure to sweep you off your feet! *Arriba* means "up".

3 oz Cruzan Single Barrel Rum

½ oz Homemade Black Pepper Syrup

1 oz Passionfruit Syrup (Torani or Monin)

5 shakes of Angostura Bitters

1½ oz Freshly Squeezed Lemon Juice

½ oz Club Soda Water

TO SERVE
Shake with crushed ice and serve in a lowball glass.

STRENGTH SCALE

El-Korero

Altogether, this recipe is a bold combination that should hit the sweet spot for tiki cocktail enthusiasts. It has, however, a funky pot still kick that will crush any and all notions that tropical drinks are for the timid.

1 oz Brennivin Icelandic Aquavit

2 oz Doctor Bird Jamaican Rum

1/4 oz Hamilton's Pimento Dram

1 oz Fresh Lemon Juice

1 oz Fresh Pineapple Juice

1 oz Monin Pomegranate Syrup

1/4 oz Club Soda

TO SERVE
Shake with crushed ice and serve in a tiki mug or highball glass with pineapple leaf garnish and a long curl of lemon twist.

Doctor Bird is an affordable Jamaican Rum imported to the United States by Two James Distillery in Detroit. It is 100 proof and really shines in tiki cocktails. If you must substitute something for it, make sure it has an equivalent kick. Something like Smith & Cross or Plantation O.F.T.D (Old Fashioned Traditional Dark) or Pusser's Gunpowder Proof (Black Label) might do in a pinch.

The Brennivin Aquavit has a distinctive caraway flavour so if you substitute it with another aquavit, make sure it is primarily caraway flavoured because not all of them are. Best enjoyed as you peruse and ponder the latest publication from Korero Press.

STRENGTH SCALE

Enchanted Sandy Warner

This cocktail was invented by Kelly in 2010. Sandy was the "Face of Exotica" and appeared on the first 12 Martin Denny albums. Like Sandy, this drink is beautiful, exotic, and enchanting, time and time again.

1½ oz Cruzan White Rum

1 oz Regular Lemon Hart 151 Rum

½ oz Grand Marnier Orange Liqueur

⅛ oz St Germain's Elderflower Liqueur

⅛ oz Disaronno Amaretto Liqueur

½ oz Reàl Coconut Squeeze

1½ oz Kern's Farm Guava Nectar

¼ oz Dole Pineapple Juice

1 oz Freshly Squeezed Lemon Juice

TO SERVE
Build in a shaker tin with finely crushed ice and flash blend. Pour the cocktail into a footed ice cream bowl with a mound of crushed ice. Add straw. Garnish with a passion or orchid flower and a sliver of fern.

STRENGTH SCALE

El Korero

Exotique

Exotique

This is one of Kelly's favourite cocktails. Pronounced "x-o-teak" it's as exotic as cocktails come. Dark rum, light rum, passion fruit, peach and eleven layers of flavours.

1 oz Dagger Rum or Dark Jamaican Rum

2 oz 10 Cane Rum (white rum is okay)

½ oz Christian Brothers Brandy

½ oz Chambord Raspberry Liqueur

1 oz Homemade Ancho Chili Pepper Syrup

½ oz Torani Passion Fruit Syrup

½ oz Reàl Coconut Squeeze

2 oz Kern's Farm Peach Nectar

1 oz Freshly Squeezed Lemon Juice

1 oz Freshly Squeezed Lime Juice

5 dashes of Angostura Bitters

TO SERVE
Shake with crushed ice and serve in a tall-footed ice tea or banquet style footed goblet glass. Garnish with a long pineapple leaf and flower blossom.

STRENGTH SCALE

Fez Flipper

A Trader Tom creation. Does the fez belong in the world of tiki or is it part and parcel of Middle East exoticism? This is the perfect drink to accompany that question, but as you continue to drink these, the answer may grow fuzzier and fuzzier... smooth, sweet, and a little bitter, but in a nice way.

1½ oz Plantation 3 Star White Rum

½ oz Rhum J.M. Agricole

¼ oz Aperol

1 oz Dole Pineapple Juice

½ oz Freshly Squeezed Lime Juice

½ oz BG Reynolds Passionfruit Syrup

1 dash of Fee Brothers Rhubarb Bitters

TO SERVE
Shake with crushed ice and serve in a lowball glass with a mint sprig and a pineapple chunk on a bamboo spear.

STRENGTH SCALE

Fuel Injection

Kelly grew up in the San Fernando Valley of Southern California in the 1970s and was born into a fast car family where she experienced cruising Van Nuys Boulevard and street races. Fuel Injection reminds us of the days when muscle cars and burning rubber were king.

Float Lemon Hart 151 Rum or Hamilton 151 Overproof Rum on top and get your motor running!

1½ oz Cruzan Blackstrap Rum

½ oz Appleton Reserve Jamaican Rum

1 oz Crème de Cassis Black Currant Liqueur

1½ oz Monin Pistachio Syrup

½ oz Freshly Squeezed Lemon Juice

½ oz Freshly Squeezed Lime Juice

TO SERVE
Fill a collins glass with crushed ice, add ingredients, then pour into a shaker tin and shake until cold. Pour all back into the Collins glass and add crushed ice to the top as needed. Add straw. Garnish with a mint sprig and your favourite swizzle stick.

STRENGTH SCALE

Grindhouse Grog

Grindhouse film features were well known for missing scenes due to splicing together footage. Too many of these and you may have some missing scenes in your memories! This is Kelly's personal favourite of all Tom's drinks! She likes the smell and thinks it would also make a good mens' cologne.

½ oz Homemade Black Pepper Syrup

½ oz Honey Syrup

1 oz Hum Liqueur

1½ oz Kraken Spiced Rum

1 oz Freshly Squeezed Lime Juice

TO SERVE
Shake with crushed ice and serve in a brandy snifter.

STRENGTH SCALE

Grindhouse Grog

Hex

Hex

This cocktail was created by Kelly for Tiki Oasis 2013's Hulabilly theme. The room she bartended was Boozin' on the Bayou sponsored by Jasmin Luna, John-O Productions and Zacapa Rum. Kelly dressed as a Voodoo Priestess, rattled the bones, told fortunes and put a HEX on party-goers! When she served it at La Descarga, Hex was served as below with ½ oz both of hibiscus and prickly pear syrups.

2 oz Zacapa Rum

½ oz Freshly Squeezed Lemon Juice

¼ tsp Clement Creole Shrub

⅓ oz Homemade Hibiscus Syrup

⅓ oz Homemade Prickly Pear Syrup

¼ oz Homemade Pimento Allspice Syrup

¼ oz Orgeat Almond Syrup

3 drops Fee Brothers Aztec Chocolate Bitters

TO SERVE
Build in a shaker tin with crushed ice. Pour cocktail into a chilled coupe. Add a dollop of Zacapa Foam (see page 243) to the top of the cocktail and sprinkle with shaved dark chocolate.

STRENGTH SCALE

The Hibiscus Hula

Tom first attempted to make this cocktail at the Rumpus Room during the spring of 2009. He then improved and simplified the drink and came up with the recipe below to serve at Tiki Oasis. It was a hit. Jeremy Fleener, the owner of the Tonga Hut in North Hollywood, even put it on their menu. It's light, and refreshing, and probably Tom's best-known cocktail.

1 oz Freshly Squeezed Lemon juice

¾ oz Freshly Squeezed Lime Juice

¼ oz BG Reynolds Orgeat Almond Syrup

¼ oz Crème de Banana Schnapps (99 Bananas)

1 oz Homemade Hibiscus Syrup

1 oz Cruzan Estate Light Rum

¾ oz Cruzan Estate Dark Rum

5 oz Crushed Ice

1 oz Club Soda

TO SERVE
Pour the ingredients into a shaker tin. Shake with crushed ice and serve in a lowball/double rocks glass. Garnish with a hibiscus flower and an umbrella.

STRENGTH SCALE

Hipalicious

A Hiphipahula signature cocktail because it's one of the first rum cocktails Kelly created years ago, and still loves. Deep dark rum topped with Lemon Hart 151 Rum. It's both sweet and tart with citrus flavours.

2 oz Appleton 12 Year Dark Rum

½ oz Orange Curaçao/Grand Marnier liqueur

2 tbsp Dark Brown Sugar (pure cane is better)

1 oz Freshly Squeezed Lemon Juice

1 oz Freshly Squeezed Lime Juice

½ oz Freshly Squeezed Orange Juice

Float of Lemon Hart 151 Rum (optional)

TO SERVE
Dissolve brown sugar thoroughly with lime and lemon juice, swirled in a shaker, then add other components and shake with crushed ice. Served tall in a highball or your favourite tiki mug. Garnish with a paper umbrella speared through a cherry, a pineapple chunk, and a lime wedge.

STRENGTH SCALE

Hoodoo Doll

This cocktail is inspired by a drink Tom once had at the now defunct Voodoo Room, which opened in West Hollywood in 2006 but lasted only one year. Rob, the bartender and co-owner, made a version called the "Voodoo Doll" (but his cocktail used only ginger syrup without Lemon Hart 151 Rum or Ginger Beer). Rob was a whirling dervish of energy and often created one-off tropical cocktails with whatever fruit happened to be in season. This drink is light, sweet, and refreshing.

1 oz Homemade Ginger Syrup

2 oz Unsweetened or Fresh Pineapple Juice

2 oz Vanilla Cruzan Rum

½ oz Lemon Hart 151 Rum

½ oz Lemon Juice and the Shell from Half Lemon

½ oz Ginger Beer

TO SERVE
Shake all ingredients, minus the ginger beer, with crushed ice and pour into a footed pilsner glass, then add the ginger beer to top. Stir gently so as not to kill the carbonation, and serve.

STRENGTH SCALE

Hipalicious

Hoodoo Hut Cocktail

Hoodoo Drummer

Tom invented this drink at the Lothario Lounge, GeeDavee's home bar in Pasadena, California. Located in a mid-century apartment complex and decorated with mod furnishings and GeeDavee's tiki carvings, entering the Lothario lounge is like stepping back in time. This particular cocktail was created on the night of a terrible windstorm in 2012 that made the national news. With the constant gusts of wind and branches knocking on the window, it really did feel like the drums were playing outside, hence the name "Hoodoo Drummer."

½ oz Marie Brizzard Pear Liqueur

1 oz Kern's Farm Mango Nectar

1 oz Freshly Squeezed Lime Juice

¼ oz Cointreau Orange Liqueur

1 oz Appleton Dark Rum

TO SERVE
Build in a shaker tin with crushed ice, shake and serve in a lowball glass.

STRENGTH SCALE

Hoodoo Hut Cocktail

The Hoodoo Hut is Tom's house drink for his home bar. It uses a blend of rums purposely meant to resemble the Jamaican Dagger Rum Blend once marketed by Wray and Nephew. *Tiki Central* has a couple of great threads about trying to recapture Dagger flavour, with tips from Hurricane Hayward, Craig "Colonel Tiki" Hermann and Martin Cate. These tips, along with actually sampling some Dagger Punch Rum (Thanks, Anders) were a huge inspiration. Dagger was the go-to rum for serious drinkers of the 1940s, '50s and '60s. Robert Mitchum notoriously drank quite a bit of it during his "Calypso Phase", and Dagger has a well-deserved dyed-in-the-wool badass reputation. The lime and orgeat are comforting components from a traditional Mai Tai. However, the Pimento Dram wakes things up with some additional spice and harkens back to Dagger's Jamaican roots.

1 oz El Dorado 12 Year Old Demerara Rum

1 oz Smith and Cross Jamaican Rum

¼ oz Lemon Hart 151 Rum

1 oz Juice and Shell from 1 Lime

1 tsp Pimento Dram Allspice Liqueur

1 oz BG Reynolds Orgeat Almond Syrup

TO SERVE
Add the ingredients to a shaker tin. Add some crushed ice and shake, then pour into a lowball glass and garnish with a mint sprig.

STRENGTH SCALE

Hula in the Dark

Tom invented this at Kevin and Claudia Murphy's Waikiki Womb Home Bar in Glendale, California. The 5-Spice Syrup was originally brought in to experiment with by Eric October. The beautiful thing about hula in the dark is that nobody can tell you're not keeping your eyes on the dancer's hands.

2 oz Cruzan Blackstrap Rum

1¼ oz Rhum Barbancourt

1 oz Homemade Chinese 5-Spice Syrup (Falernum can be used as a substitute)

¼ oz BG Reynolds Orgeat Almond Syrup

1 oz Kern's Farm Passionfruit Nectar

1 oz Freshly Squeezed Lemon Juice

1 oz Freshly Squeezed Lime Juice

½ oz Club Soda Water

TO SERVE
Shake with crushed ice. Serve tall or in your tiki mug with a hibiscus blossom garnish.

STRENGTH SCALE

Ivre Poire (Drunken Pear)

Created by Kelly and premiered at La Descarga in Los Angeles, California. Go ahead and give in to pear pressure and taste this un-pear-ably delicious cocktail that will take you to pear-adise!

2½ oz Clement V.S.O.P Rum or 6 year Clement

1 oz Marie Brizard Pear William Liqueur

½ oz Drambuie Honey Liqueur

½ oz Honey Mix (heat equal parts of honey and water and cool)

½ oz Freshly Squeezed Lemon Juice

TO SERVE
Shake in a shaker tin with crushed ice, then pour into a chilled champagne coupe. Garnish with a very thin slice of Anjou pear.

STRENGTH SCALE

Hula in the Dark

Kauai Island Jungle Sling

Jumpin' Jezebel

Created by Tom. This flavour combination is inspired by a Southern jam recipe. Try to get unfiltered and unpasteurized apple cider if possible. There are some great local varieties out there, and different ciders could make for very different versions. My current favourite is "Honey Crisp" but go out and visit your orchards and farmer's markets to see what's available. Meet some people while you're at it and invite them back to try your cocktail creations.

1½ oz Plantation Three Star Light Rum

1 oz Fresh Pineapple Juice

1½ oz Fresh Apple Cider

½ oz Freshly Squeezed Lemon Juice

¼ oz Ancho Reyes Liqueur

TO SERVE
Shake with crushed ice and strain into a chilled coupe glass with a big cube of ice. Garnish with a thin sliver of apple draped over the cube.

STRENGTH SCALE

Kauai Island Jungle Sling

Based on a traditional Singapore Sling, this version of Tom's trades out the gin for a quality white rum and replaces the cherry liqueur with a lighter dose of cherry syrup. It also replaces the grenadine with pomegranate liqueur.

1 oz Plantation 3 Star White Rum

1 oz El Dorado 12 Year Old Rum

¼ oz Yellow Chartreuse

¼ oz PAMA Pomegranate Liqueur

½ oz Cherry Syrup

¼ oz Orange Cointreau

1½ oz Unsweetened Pineapple Juice

½ oz Freshly Squeezed Lime Juice

1 dash of Angostura Bitters

TO SERVE
Add all liquids and shake with crushed ice, pour into a piña colada glass, then garnish with a speared chunk of fresh pineapple and a pitted cherry.

STRENGTH SCALE

Kekō Mōkaki (Monkey Mess)

Kelly created this in true island spirit, slightly creamy, with a nice touch of the sweet and a splash of the exotic. Here is a Polynesian fact for you — Did you know there are no monkeys in Polynesia? They are not native to Polynesia. In tiki culture, we often celebrate monkeys because... well heck, they are fun, and they wear fezzes. Kekō Mōkaki is what happens when the monkeys are let loose to wreak havoc.

1½ oz Cruzan Coconut Rum

1½ oz Castries Peanut Liqueur

1 oz Godiva Chocolate Liqueur

½ oz Banana Liqueur

TO SERVE

Build in a shaker tin. Shake with crushed ice and serve in a lidded coconut monkey mug or container of choice. Garnish with banana.

STRENGTH SCALE

Kelly's Quintessential Rum Barrel (KQRB)

TOP SECRET

This is Kelly's delicious take on an old standard. Sorry, we can't tell you the actual ingredients. However, it is a proprietary recipe currently under negotiation to be listed on a well-known commercial tiki bar menu. Hopefully available for you to try out soon. It is truly delicious! We included it here, not to tease you but so that all of her recipes are represented. If you are still thirsty for a rum barrel in the meantime, you could try Trader Tom's Wayward Rum Barrel (see page 144) which is entirely different.

Since the beginning, most Polynesian restaurants and tiki bars have had some variant of a rum barrel cocktail on their menus. In general, most use a couple of different juices, some Jamaican rum, and garnish with lots of mint, but that still leaves lots of room for innovation. In fact, there are probably hundreds of vintage recipes out there. They could even be collected into their own book — *The Big Book Of Rum Barrels!*

STRENGTH SCALE

Keko Mōkaki

Kick in the Coconuts

Kelly's Special

In 2012, during a Traveling Rumpus Room gathering at Sven Kirsten's Home in Silverlake, California, a dynamic new Hiphipahula cocktail with no name was tasted. A toast was made and Mike Buhen Senior, the owner of the Tiki Ti in Los Angeles, raised his glass and proclaimed "It's Kelly's Special!" You'll find information on Port Wine Reduction on page 243.

1 oz Coruba Dark Jamaican Rum

¼ oz St. Germain Elderflower Liqueur

¾ oz Cruzan Light Rum

2 oz "Special Summer" Port Wine Reduction

1 oz Simple Syrup

1 oz Kern's Apricot Nectar

¾ oz Freshly Squeezed Lemon Juice

TO SERVE
Shake with crushed ice and served tall in a highball or your favourite tiki mug. Garnish with a raw sugar cane swizzle and an umbrella speared through a lemon wheel.

STRENGTH SCALE

Kick In The Coconuts

A Kelly original, this seems as if it will be a delicate piña colada type drink on first sight, but the blackstrap and ancho flavours pack a bit of a wallop!

2 oz Cruzan Coconut Rum

1 oz Cruzan Blackstrap Rum

2 oz Homemade Ancho Pepper Syrup

½ oz Reàl Coconut Squeeze

½ oz Freshly Squeezed Lime Juice

TO SERVE
This delicious cocktail is shaken with crushed ice and served in a coconut mug. Garnish with a pineapple leaf and a spear on the side decorated with a cherry, a pineapple, and a lime.

STRENGTH SCALE

Kilauea Sizzle

A Kelly cocktail. With Dark Jamaican Rum and a delicate suggestion of vanilla fruits and spices. When the soul of the Hawaiian fire goddess, Pele, collides with the demigod, Kamapua'a, the volcano Kīlauea sizzles. That's romance for you!

2 oz Dark Jamaican Rum

2 oz Licor 43

½ oz Homemade Ancho Chili Syrup

½ oz Freshly Squeezed Lime Juice

A splash of Soda Water

TO SERVE
Prepare in a collins glass with crushed ice, then transfer to a shaker and flash blend or shake vigorously. Pour back into a collins glass. Garnish with a lime wedge and cherries on a pick.

STRENGTH SCALE

The Koenig

Pierre Koenig is one of the 20th century's most influential architects, known for his modernist style glass and steel structures, particularly the Stahl House in the Hollywood Hills. In this spirit, Kelly delivers a modern cocktail for a refined palate.

2 oz Clement Vieux V.S.O.P. Rhum

½ oz St. Germain Elderflower Liqueur

⅛ oz Velvet Falernum

½ oz Freshly Squeezed Lime Juice

½ oz Freshly Squeezed Lemon Juice

1 oz Homemade Rhubarb Syrup

½ oz Appleton 12 Year Dark Rum

TO SERVE
Serve ungarnished in a sleek modern-stemmed glass.

STRENGTH SCALE

The Koenig

Kon-Tiki Rain

Kon-Tiki Rain

This was invented by Kelly and Tom in 2009. We didn't have a name for it when it was first made at Grog's (Ernie Keen's) during a travelling Rumpus Room. The following weekend, however, at the Tonga Hut in North Hollywood, Elvis Presley's "Cold Kentucky Rain" was on and Grog suggested the name "Kon-Tiki Rain" as a humorous riff, and the name stuck.

1 oz Cruzan Vanilla Rum

2 oz Barbancourt (three-star) Rum

1½ oz Domaine de Canton Ginger Liqueur

2 oz Orgeat Almond Syrup

¼ oz Homemade Pimento Allspice syrup

1½ oz Freshly Squeezed Lemon Juice

1 oz Freshly Squeezed Lime Juice

A splash of Club Soda

A float of Lemon Hart 151 Rum

TO SERVE
Shake with crushed ice and serve in a large tiki mug. Garnish with fresh mint sprigs and a spear with a cherry, a lemon wedge and a lime wedge. Either the mug or bowl version can be lit on fire using a half lime shell with a sugar cube coated with a small amount of Lemon Hart 151 Overproof Rum or lemon juice extract. For a fire show, sprinkle a small amount of dusted cinnamon powder and watch the sparks fly!

STRENGTH SCALE

Kona's Curse

A sacred potion born of Gilligan's Island's volcano. If you dare, step into the quicksand of Lemon Hart 151, El Dorado Demerara and Appleton Rums. Sure to make the ground beneath your feet quake! A Kelly special you are not soon to forget. It premiered at the Gilligan's Island Three Hour Tour Art Show in 2010.

1 oz 151 Lemon Hart 151 Rum

1 oz Demerara Rum 80 Proof
(Lemon Hart or El Dorado)

1 oz Appleton v/x Rum

¼ oz Kahlúa Coffee Liqueur

¼ oz Crème de Noyaux

1 dash of Pimento Liqueur

¼ oz Homemade Ancho Pepper Syrup

⅓ oz Kern's Farm Guava Nectar

½ oz Freshly Squeezed Lime Juice

½ oz Freshly Squeezed Lemon Juice

½ oz White Grapefruit Juice

TO SERVE
Serve in footed pilsner glass or a tiki mug. Garnish with tiki swizzle stick and a lime wedge.

STRENGTH SCALE

Kupa Kai Swizzle

"Swizzle me this, swizzle me that?" OOPS! Wrong '60s TV series. This was created by Kelly and premiered at the Gilligan's Island Three Hour Tour Art Show in 2010, but it kicks with a "ZOW!" and "WHAM!" that Batman would be impressed by.

1 oz 151 Demerara Rum
(Lemon Hart 151 suggested)

1 oz Demerara Rum 80 proof
(Lemon Hart suggested)

½ oz Crème de Noyaux

½ Pomegranate Syrup (Torani brand)

¾ Freshly Squeezed Lime Juice

¼ oz Cinnamon Syrup (Torani brand)

A splash of Soda Water

A dusting of Nutmeg

TO SERVE
Build in a rocks glass. Grate some nutmeg on top. Garnish with a lime wedge and a rock candy swizzle stick.

STRENGTH SCALE

The Lazy Lei

This is a Tom cocktail that bears some DNA from a Dark 'n' Stormy cocktail but takes a bit of a detour.

1 oz Blackwell's Jamaican Rum

1½ oz Lost Spirits Polynesian Style Cask Strength Rum

1 oz Freshly Squeezed Lime Juice

½ oz BG Reynolds Orgeat Almond Syrup

2½ oz Fever-Tree Ginger Beer

3 drops Bitterman's Elemakule Tiki Bitters

TO SERVE
Shake with crushed ice and serve in a rocks/old fashioned glass. Garnish with a lime wedge on the rim of the glass.

STRENGTH SCALE

Kupa Kai Swizzle

Little Buddy

Lights Out

This drink was inspired by the Stealth Cocktail at the Tiki-Ti, (which includes Kahlúa, Lemon Hart 151 Overproof Rum, Amaretto, Grand Marnier, and Bailey's Irish Cream). This is one of their strongest, if not THE STRONGEST, drinks at the Ti. It goes down smoothly because of the cream liqueur and can be more deadly than a Zombie, which telegraphs its punch much better. Tom made this variation at Murph's Waikiki Womb Home Bar in Glendale, California, at the request of Jeremy Fleener (owner of Tonga Hut). The 5-Spice Syrup was originally brought in for him to experiment with by Eric October. This is what The Dude (The Big Lebowski) would drink if he went on vacation in Jamaica and they were out of vodka to make his usual White Russian.

2 oz Lemon Hart 151 Rum

1 oz Amarula Cream Liqueur

1 oz Kahlúa Coffee Liqueur

1 oz Grand Marnier

1 oz Homemade Chinese 5-Spice Syrup
(Falernum can substitute)

TO SERVE
Shake with crushed ice. Add an orange wheel garnish on the side.

STRENGTH SCALE

Little Buddy

A Kelly castaway cocktail, which premiered at the Gilligan's Island Three Hour Tour Art Show in 2010. Your best friend when stranded on a desert island. A tall and frosty cascade of tropical flavours.

1 oz Cruzan Coconut Rum

1 oz Cruzan Mango Rum

½ oz Chambord Raspberry Liqueur

½ oz Kern's Farm Guava Nectar

½ oz Coco Reàl Squeeze

1 oz Freshly Squeezed Lemon Juice

½ oz Freshly Squeezed Lime Juice

½ oz Dole Pineapple Juice

A float dark Jamaican rum

TO SERVE
Build in a shaker tin and flash blend, then pour into a footed pilsner or a tiki mug. Garnish with an umbrella, a cherry, a pineapple wedge and a lime wedge.

STRENGTH SCALE

Luau Pig

Invented by Kelly & Tom in 2009 at Kirby & Polly's Rumpus Room in La Crescenta, California. With the apple and smoke flavours, it lives up to its name. To see the bowl version of Luau Pig, flip forward to pages 226–227.

1 dash of Angostura Bitters

1¾ oz Homemade Black Pepper Syrup

1 oz Homemade Hibiscus Syrup

¼ oz Cinnamon Syrup

1½ oz Apple Juice

½ oz John D. Taylor's Falernum

1 oz Pineapple Juice

1 oz Martinique or White Rum

1 oz Freshly Squeezed Lime Juice

1½ oz Lemon Hart 80 Proof Rum

1 oz Club Soda

TO SERVE

Shake with crushed ice and serve in a very large tiki mug or small tiki chalice or bowl. Garnish with apple slices. For added flavour, you could even cut your apple slices ahead of time and jar them up with Bakon Vodka for a few weeks, or substitute 1 oz Bakon Vodka for the White Rum to go the whole hog.

STRENGTH SCALE

Lulu Kai (Calm Sea)

This is a Kelly and Tom cocktail that was made at the Rumpus Room in La Crescenta, California, using Tom's homemade chamomile syrup. Someone joked that chamomile always makes them sleepy, so we christened this drink the "Calm Sea" or "Lulu Kai."

2 oz Diplomatico Reserve Blanco (White) Rum

½ oz Homemade Black Pepper Syrup

1 oz Domaine de Canton Ginger Liqueur

1½ oz Freshly Squeezed Lemon Juice

2 oz White Grapefruit Juice

1 oz Homemade Chamomile Syrup

TO SERVE

Shake with crushed ice and garnish rim with kumquat on a pick that's been carved to look like a goldfish.

STRENGTH SCALE

Lulu Kai

Makakoa Kelek

Makakoa Kelekele

Inspired by the Painkiller cocktail but with extra punch and even more island flavours to dull the pain. Made by Kelly for *Tiki Night* at La Descarga in Los Angeles. *Makakoa Kelekele* is Hawaiian for "Fierce Mudslide".

1 oz Smith & Cross Overproof Jamaican Rum

½ oz Appleton 12 Year Jamaican Dark

½ oz Cointreau Orange Liqueur

1 oz St. Elizabeth's Pimento Allspice Dram

½ oz Freshly Squeezed Lime Juice

½ oz Orange Juice

1 oz Pineapple Juice

1 oz Coco Reàl Squeeze

A float of Demerara 151 Rum
(Lemon Hart or Hamilton)

TO SERVE
Build cocktail and flash blend with crushed ice, then pour into a footed pilsner or a tiki mug, and float 151 rum. Grate fresh nutmeg on top. Garnish with a pineapple spear and leaf.

STRENGTH SCALE

Malaysian Holiday

This is the perfect cocktail to make before sitting down to watch Bob Hope and Bing Crosby in the classic 1940 American comedy film, *Road To Singapore*. This is also worth the time to make the sesame syrup. Kelly rates this as one of Tom's top 5 cocktails!

¾ oz Homemade Sesame Syrup

¼ oz Cinnamon Syrup

1 oz Cruzan Coconut Rum

1½ oz Freshly Squeezed Lemon Juice

1 oz El Dorado 12-Year-Old Demerara Rum

1 oz Kern's Farm Guava Nectar

TO SERVE
Shake with crushed ice and serve in a lowball glass. Garnish with a raw sugar cane swizzle stick and a couple of "fireball" cherries (see pages 239–240) speared through on a paper umbrella.

STRENGTH SCALE

Manakooran Moonbeam

This was invented by Tom at Kirby & Polly's Rumpus Room in La Crescenta, California. The pineapple can be substituted with already crushed pineapple, but he used a muddler and then a few seconds on high with an old Hamilton shake mixer to get the right consistency. This drink was named for the song, "Moon over Manakoora" about a mythical south sea island paradise. Have one or two of these and sail away.

3 oz Kern's Farm Guava Nectar

2 oz Freshly Squeezed Lemon Juice

½ oz BG Reynolds Orgeat Almond Syrup

½ oz Monin Blood Orange Syrup

½ oz Senior's Brand Orange Curaçao

3 Pulped Pineapple Rings

1 squirt of Coco Reàl or tsp Coco López

2 oz St. Germain Elderflower Liqueur

2 oz Coruba Dark Jamaican Rum

5 oz Crushed Ice

TO SERVE
Shake with crushed ice and served tall in your favourite tiki mug or hurricane glass. Garnish with a pineapple wedge on a skewer with a tall pineapple leaf sticking out.

STRENGTH SCALE

Mauna Poli'Ahu

This is a Kelly cocktail/cordial inspired by the Hawaiian gods, Poli'Ahu, one of the four Hawaiian goddesses of snow, and Pele, the goddess of fire. According to legend, they are locked in an eternal battle over the island of Hawai'i — with Pele ruling over the fiery southern end of the island and Poli'Ahu ruling over the snowy northern end.

1 oz Zaya Dark Rum

2 muddled Fresh Raspberries

5 muddled Raisins

¾ oz Honey Syrup

5 drops Fee Brothers Aztec Chocolate Bitters

⅛ Chambord Raspberry Liqueur

1 dash of Clement Creole Shrubb

¼ oz Orange Juice

You need to macerate the raisins in a teaspoon of Zaya at room temperature for half an hour or so to make them plump enough to muddle before you are ready to mix.

TO SERVE
Build in a tin and muddle the fruit. Shake with crushed ice and then fine strain into a brandy snifter. Place a large ice cube in the centre and top with a 151 overproof soaked raspberry before lighting on fire.

STRENGTH SCALE

Manakooran Moonbeam

Mele Kalikimaka Mock Martini

Mary Ann's Homemade Coconut Cream Pie

"Is that pie I smell in the window of that hut?" From the farms of Kansas to the sands of Hawaii comes Mary Ann's own liquid delight. Kelly created this for the Gilligan's Island Three Hour Tour Art Show in 2010.

2 oz Cruzan Coconut Rum

1 oz Coco Reàl Squeeze

1½ oz Freshly Squeezed Lemon Juice

TO SERVE
Build in a short hurricane glass (colada glass) with crushed ice and then transfer to a tin and flash blend (5 seconds) before pouring back into the glass.

STRENGTH SCALE

Mele Kalikimaka Mock Martini

Created by Kelly in Christmas 2009. On a Bright Hawaiian Christmas day Godiva White Chocolate Liquor can evoke the soft glow of powdery snow warmed in the tropics with Coconut Rum. Serve strained straight up, with a peppermint swizzle. A real holiday treat.

1½ oz Cruzan Coconut Rum

1 oz Godiva White Chocolate Liqueur

1 oz Monin Pumpkin Spice Syrup

⅛ oz Maraschino Cherry Syrup

TO SERVE
Serve in a sugar-rimmed martini glass.

STRENGTH SCALE

Menehune's Kiss

Created at Kirby and Polly's Rumpus Room in La Crescenta, California. Tom created the chamomile syrup and brought it that night with the intent of inventing some new cocktails, and he and Kelly came up with this. This drink has such a light and delicate flavour that they named it after the Menehune (Hawaiian Elves) whose mysterious ways are hard to fathom, but whose magic is legendary.

2 oz Diplomatico Blanco (White) Reserve Rum

1 oz Appleton 12 Year Dark Jamaican Rum

1 oz Domaine de Canton Ginger Liqueur

1 oz Homemade Chamomile Syrup

1 oz Kern's Farm Peach Nectar

1 oz Freshly Squeezed Lime Juice

1 oz Freshly Squeezed Lemon Juice

A splash of Soda Water

TO SERVE
Serve in a large tiki mug or small tiki bowl. Garnish with a slice of peach on the rim.

STRENGTH SCALE

Moai Madness

This was created by Tom and Kelly, originally for the 2011 Moai Madness Art Show, but saw further refinement and change until they settled on the current recipe. Rums, liqueurs and the flavours of the island evoke a lingering breeze, but can bring a moai to his knees!

1 oz Kōloa Kaua'i Dark Hawaiian Rum

1 oz Smith and Cross Jamaican Rum

½ oz Hum Liqueur

1 oz Grade A Maple Syrup

1 oz Freshly Squeezed Lemon Juice

A splash of Soda Water

TO SERVE
Shake with crushed ice and serve in a double rocks Old Fashioned Glass. Garnish with a long strip of lemon peel and a raw sugar cane swizzle stick.

STRENGTH SCALE

Moai Madness

Mug Cracker

Monk-ey Nut

This drink was created by Kelly and is ten layers of fun. This is what happens when the Frangelico Monk's pet monkey escapes the monastery, mixing their precious liqueurs with island flavours without regard for rules or sacred vows. Hide your children when the Monk-ey is on the loose!

½ oz Cruzan Light (White) Rum

1¼ oz Cruzan Coconut Rum

¼ oz Frangelico Hazelnut Liqueur

½ oz Coco Reàl Squeeze

½ oz Homemade Ancho Pepper Syrup

1½ oz Kern's Farm Guava Nectar

¼ oz Torani Passionfruit Syrup

¾ oz Freshly Squeezed Lime Juice

A splash of Soda Water

A float of Demerara Rum (80 proof)

TO SERVE
Served tall in a hurricane glass or your favourite tiki mug. Garnish with a tall pineapple leaf and a couple of raw sugar cane sticks.

STRENGTH SCALE

Mug Cracker

This was introduced at Kevin and Claudia Murphy's Waikiki Womb in Glendale, California. Invented by Kelly and Tom, who asked everyone there to try a couple of different versions and then they finally decided on their favourite combination. This was one of our first uses of our cracked black pepper syrup. Don't use your expensive mugs for this one. You've been warned!

1 oz Homemade Sweet and Sour Syrup

1 oz Homemade Cracked Black Pepper Syrup

1 oz Reàl Coconut Squeeze

1 oz Plantation O.F.T.D.

1 oz Appleton White Rum

1¾ oz Club Soda

TO SERVE
Add crushed ice to taste, flash blend, and serve in a lowball glass or a tiki mug. Garnish with a lime and cherry on a spear.

STRENGTH SCALE

Mystique Noir

A Kelly and Tom recipe, inspired by several coffee grogs, including the Mai-Kai restaurant's legendary Black Magic.

1 oz Blackwell Jamaican Rum

1 oz Appleton 12 Year Dark Rum

1 oz Brinley's Gold Dark Vanilla Rum

½ oz St. Elizabeth Pimento Allspice Dram

1 oz Fresh Orange Juice

¾ oz White Grapefruit Juice

½ oz Grand Marnier Orange Liqueur

2 oz Dark Espresso Coffee

½ oz Freshly Squeezed Lemon Juice

¼ oz Torani Cinnamon Syrup

1 oz Torani Salted Caramel Syrup

TO SERVE
Blend in blender with about 2 cups of crushed ice and serve in a brandy snifter with orange peel on top and a dusting of cinnamon.

STRENGTH SCALE

Peanut Mug Salute!

This is a riff by Trader Tom on the old southern favourite of including peanuts in bottles of Coca Cola to add a little extra flavour.

1¾ oz El Dorado 12 Year Demerara Rum

1 oz Homemade Peanut Orgeat (see appendices)

Coca-Cola (Mexican version/Cane Sugar version)

TO SERVE
Build in a tall pint glass with crushed ice and top add cola to the top of the glass. Gently stir with a bartender spoon so as not to destroy the carbonation. If possible, to be served in the classic vintage "Peanut Mug" put out by PMP (Paul Marshall Products) in the 1960s. Garnish with a large shelled and dry roasted/salted peanut floating on top. If you want your peanut cocktail a bit more salted, you can salt the rim beforehand by wetting the top edge of your mug and rolling it in salt. If you want to experiment with a bit more of a herbal flavour, you might try Fentiman's Curiosity Cola in place of the Coca-Cola.

STRENGTH SCALE

Mystique Noir

Pele's Passion

Pele's Kiss

This drink in honour of Pele, the Hawaiian fire goddess, and daughter of Haumea, the earth mother, was originally conceived as a bowl drink by Kelly. You can find the scaled-up recipe on page 229.

1 oz Cruzan Coconut Rum

½ oz Cruzan Vanilla Rum

1 oz Homemade Ancho Pepper Syrup

1 oz Cracked Black Pepper Syrup

⅛ oz Disaronno Almond Liqueur

½ oz Lemon Hart 151 Rum

½ oz Orange Juice

½ oz Freshly Squeezed Lime Juice

TO SERVE

Shake with crushed ice and serve in a chalice or a tiki mug. Garnish with one half of a Dragon Fruit that has the leaves licking upwards to mimic flames. Place a sugar cube soaked in overproof rum or lemon extract at the top of the leaves and light on fire. Shower with cinnamon powder for sparks! All hail Pele! Her kiss is on fire then tempered with cool love. The sweet Rums, coconut and vanilla come together but not for long, Pele is angry, and with this anger comes Lemon Hart 151 Rum. Sweetness is spun into a unique spicy cocktail you must savour. Pele's Kiss is tantalising!

STRENGTH SCALE

Pele's Passion

This was invented by Tom at Kirby and Polly's Rumpus Room in La Crescenta, California. The volcano goddess is a harsh mistress to those who do not heed her desires. With liberal doses of both passionfruit nectar and exotic spices, this is sure to keep her satisfied. Keep extra crushed ice on hand, just in case her fire becomes an inferno!

2 oz Cruzan White Rum

½ oz Lemon Hart 80 Proof Rum

¾ oz Curaçao Orange Liqueur

1 oz Domaine de Canton Ginger Liqueur

4 oz Kern's Farm Passionfruit Nectar

1 oz Freshly Squeezed Lime Juice

¼ oz Homemade Black Pepper Syrup

1 oz BG Reynolds Orgeat Almond Syrup

A splash of Club Soda

TO SERVE

Shake with crushed ice and serve in your favourite tiki mug. Garnish with an orange wedge on a spear.

STRENGTH SCALE

Persian Carpet Ride

Created by Trader Tom. These traditional exotic flavours will take you on a magic carpet ride to leave your cares behind. You can buy dry rose petals from Middle Eastern grocery stores and make your own simple syrup with them if you choose. It could also be the perfect way to repurpose that romantic bouquet for a stay-at-home vacation. There are also commercial brands of rose syrup available. The herbal Chartreuse cuts through the sweet rose syrup and blends with the rich walnut liqueur.

1 oz Rose Syrup

¼ oz Walnut Liqueur

½ oz Yellow Chartreuse Liqueur

1 oz Freshly Squeezed Lemon Juice

2 oz Plantation 3 Star Light Rum

TO SERVE
Shake with crushed ice and then add a liberal splash of soda water and stir in. Serve in a glass chalice with mint leaves and rose petals.

STRENGTH SCALE

Phuket Phizz

Pronounced "poo'ket fiz." Effervescent with exotic flavours this drink was created at Kirby's Rumpus Room in La Crescenta, California, in 2010. Tom was inspired to use some Thai flavours, and this drink was created after many previous attempts that were thoroughly tested by the crowd that was present. One of our Rumpus Room regulars loved this drink so much, he went home and made his own syrup blend that was equal parts lemongrass, black pepper, and ginger, so that he could make the drink faster!

1½ oz Homemade Lemongrass Syrup

1 oz Homemade Black Pepper Syrup

1 oz BG Reynolds or Homemade Ginger Syrup

2 oz Coruba Dark Jamaican Rum

1 oz Cruzan Coconut Rum

2 oz Kern's Farm Mango Nectar

2 oz Freshly Squeezed Lime Juice

A splash of Soda Water

5 oz Crushed Ice

TO SERVE
Shake with crushed ice and serve in a colada or hurricane glass. Garnish with a paper umbrella and Pitted Cherry.

STRENGTH SCALE

Phuket Phizz

Pohō Moku

Pirate Girl's Sea Shanty

This is Trader Tom's wife's favourite cocktail. It's very light and easy to make. Tom invented it at the Hoodoo Hut, Tom's home bar.

Before Facebook, tiki aficionados spent much of their time on Hanford Lemoore's website, *Tiki Central*. It's still maintained to this day and is a great repository of cocktail and other information. To join the site, you have to come up with a catchy *Tiki Central* name and Tom's wife's was "Pirate Girl". The name never really stuck but at least the recipe proved a success!

2 oz Kern's Farm Guava Nectar

2 oz Unsweetened Pineapple Juice

1 oz Freshly Squeezed Lime Juice

1½ oz Cruzan Coconut Rum

TO SERVE
Add all the liquids and shake with crushed ice, then garnish with a speared chunk of fresh pineapple and a pitted cherry.

STRENGTH SCALE

Pohō Moku

Can also be served in a small drinking bowl. Often served on fire using a half spent lime shell with sugar cube coated with a small amount of 151 overproof rum or lemon juice extract. For a fire show, sprinkle a small amount of dusted cinnamon powder and watch the sparks fly! Created by Kelly. Evokes a lingering breeze from the islands.

3 oz Cruzan Vanilla Rum

1 oz Grand Marnier Orange Liqueur

1 oz Domaine de Canton Ginger Liqueur

1 oz Homemade Ancho Chili Pepper Syrup

½ oz Torani Passionfruit Syrup

1½ oz Freshly Squeezed Lemon Juice

1½ oz Freshly Squeezed Lime Juice

2 oz Soda Water

TO SERVE
Shake with crushed ice and served in a wide-bowled and stemmed cocktail glass. Garnish with lime and cherries on a spear.

STRENGTH SCALE

Polynesian Headsplitter

Created by Trader Tom, this is a more powerful drink than the initial 2½ oz of rum `might suggest. It's made with Lost Spirits 66% ABV cask strength rum (132 Proof). If that's too difficult to obtain, you can substitute 2 oz of Plantation O.F.T.D. (138 Proof), or 2 oz of a 151 rum like Lemon Hart or Hamilton along with half an oz of Stiggin's Fancy Pineapple Rum for the lower ABV and fruity profile.

2½ oz Lost Spirits Polynesian Style Rum

1 oz Freshly Squeezed Lime Juice

1 oz Freshly Squeezed Pineapple Juice

1 oz Homemade Sesame Syrup

2 dashes of Bitterman's Elamakule Tiki Bitters

3 Leaves of Mint, muddled

TO SERVE
Shake with crushed ice and serve in a lowball glass. Garnish with a large "war club" swizzle of rock candy.

STRENGTH SCALE

Pomegranate Pygmy

Tom created this cocktail, specifically, for the 2007 Tiki Oasis Drink Crawl. It was a big hit. Originally he used DeKuyper Pomegranate Schnapps but later deferred to the more expensive PAMA Pomegranate Liqueur as a tastier alternative.

Careful, this is one pygmy that packs a punch!

4 oz Kern's Farm Guava Nectar

¾ oz Freshly Squeezed Lime Juice

2 oz PAMA Pomegranate Liqueur

2 oz Cruzan Light Rum

4 oz Crushed Ice

TO SERVE
Flash blend for five seconds and serve in a lowball glass. Garnish with a couple of pitted cherries on an umbrella and a mint sprig.

STRENGTH SCALE

Polynesian Headsplitter

Punji Stick

Punji Stick

This drink has a surprisingly strong rum flavour despite having less than 2 oz of rum. Of course, the Polynesian Rum is overproof at 66% and imparts strong flavour, counterbalanced by the richness of the Appleton. A Trader Tom original created in the Hoodoo Hut, West Hills location.

This drink's closest relative would be the classic "Polynesian Paralysis" which was made with Sweet and Sour mix instead of just lime juice and with Okolehao (Hawaiian Whiskey).

Like the sharpened wood Punji stick traps that American veterans encountered in the jungles during the Vietnam war, this drink is sneaky and can do some real damage if you're not careful!

2½ oz Simply brand Orange with Pineapple Juice

1 oz Liquid Alchemist Orgeat Syrup

1 oz Freshly Squeezed Lime Juice

1½ oz Appleton 12 Year

¼ oz Lost Spirits Polynesian Rum

2 dashes of Bitterman's Elakamule Tiki Bitters

A splash of Club Soda

In lieu of Simply brand Orange with Pineapple Juice, you can simply mix one part of each of orange and pineapple juice.

TO SERVE
Shake with ice and serve in a highball glass with skewered orange slice and pineapple chunk as garnish.

STRENGTH SCALE

Professor's Nocturnal Dream

A cocktail inspired by an erotic dream. Even a buttoned-up professor can only hold his passions in check for so long! A heaping helping of ginger is just the prescription he needs. Created by Kelly and premiered at the Gilligan's Island Three Hour Tour Art Show in 2010.

2 oz Cruzan Coconut Rum

1 oz Domaine de Canton Ginger Liqueur

¾ oz Homemade Ginger Syrup

¼ oz Coco Reàl Squeeze

½ oz Kern's Farm Guava Nectar

¾ oz Freshly Squeezed Lemon Juice

½ oz Freshly Squeezed Lime Juice

TO SERVE
Build in a shaker tin and transfer to a footed pilsner.

STRENGTH SCALE

Redstone 3

A Kelly original rum punch that is ready for take-off. The launch of the Mercury-Redstone 3 (Freedom 7), placed the first American astronaut, Alan Shepard, in orbit on May 5, 1961. The launch vehicle was based on the Redstone rocket developed by the U.S. Army which had the distinction of launching the first American satellite, Explorer 1, into orbit in 1958.

2 oz Kōloa Kaua'i Dark Rum

1 oz Prickly Pear Syrup

½ oz Monin Pomegranate Syrup

½ oz Kern's Farm Guava Nectar

⅓ oz Homemade Pimento Allspice Syrup

¼ oz Coco Reàl Squeeze

¼ oz Torani Passionfruit Syrup

½ oz Freshly Squeezed Lime Juice

½ oz Orange Juice

TO SERVE
Shake with crushed ice and served in a footed pilsner glass. Garnish with a spear including a lime wedge and THREE red cherries.

STRENGTH SCALE

Rooster In The Road

Created by Kelly Hiphipahula, and inspired by a trip she took to Florida's Key West where Gypsy Roosters rule the streets. In 1970, cockfighting became illegal there and the roosters were let loose. They are permitted to roam freely and have the right of way and are considered very much a part of Key West.

½ oz Blue Curaçao

2 oz Cruzan Coconut Rum

½ oz Hum Liqueur

¼ oz Black Sambuca

1 oz Freshly Squeezed Lemon Juice

½ oz Cinnamon Syrup

TO SERVE
Mix the above with crushed ice and prepare to pour into a lowball glass, bearing in mind you want to add a layer of ½ oz Homemade Hibiscus Syrup on the bottom and float of ½ oz Cockspur Rum on the top. So, the drink will have three distinct layers and resemble the feathered plumage of Florida roosters who are always stopping traffic. Garnish with a pineapple leaf and a raw sugar cane swizzle stick.

STRENGTH SCALE

Redstone 3

Satchmo's Scat

Satchmo's Scat

Kelly's tip of the hat to the great Louis "Satchmo" Armstrong. To pay homage to the world's most famous trumpeter and New Orleanian, what is more perfect than a dousing of Old New Orleans Rums, Créole Shrub and splashes of all kinds of N'awlins in there? Grab some beaded necklaces and meet us on Bourbon Street.

1 oz Old New Orleans Light Rum

1¼ oz Old New Orleans Dark Rum

½ oz Homemade Pimento Allspice Syrup

¼ oz Clement Creole Shrub

¾ oz Homemade Prickly Pear Syrup

¾ oz Freshly Squeezed Lime Juice

TO SERVE
Mix with crushed ice and serve in a silver metal julep cup. Garnish with mint.

STRENGTH SCALE

Savage Marubi

A Kelly original from the deepest jungle to bring out the savage headhunter in you. An exotic elixir of hand-selected premium rums and liqueurs. Retrieved from the cave, hidden away by residents of the neighbouring island. Spirit this treasure away before the drumming forewarns of the headhunters' return.

1 oz Kōloa Kaua'i Spice Rum

1 oz Plantation Three Star Light Rum

½ oz Kiwi Liqueur

½ oz PAMA Pomegranate Liqueur

¾ Freshly Squeezed Lime Juice

½ oz Homemade Cracked Black Pepper Syrup

A float of Appleton Reserve Rum

TO SERVE
Shake with crushed ice and serve in an old-fashioned glass with a spent lime shell floating on top that is filled with a sugar cube coated with a dab of Lemon Hart 151 and lit on fire. Then sprinkle cinnamon on top for a shower of sparks. Careful not to singe your hula skirt!

STRENGTH SCALE

Shaka Hula Bossa Nova

The cocktail was invented through trial and error by both Tom and Kelly at the first night of a travelling Rumpus Room that met at Ernie Keen's (Grog's) home Tiki bar instead of Kirby's. Ernie was shocked to see us dump a full bucket of discarded drinks in search of a cocktail to match Kelly's concept. The final product went through several tastings and was a surprise to everyone when we settled on the final recipe. We knew it was something special and it went on to be one of Kelly's go-to drinks when she began serving it at the Tonga Hut in North Hollywood. This drink's name was inspired by the Tikiyaki Orchestra song.

1 oz Coruba Dark Jamaican Rum

1 oz Lemon Hart 151 Rum

1 oz Mount Gay Eclipse Rum

1 oz Homemade Ancho Chili Pepper Syrup

5 dashes of Angostura bitters

½ oz Christian Brothers Brandy

1 oz Torani Passionfruit Syrup

1 oz Freshly Squeezed Lemon Juice

1 oz Freshly Squeezed Lime Juice

2 oz Club Soda

TO SERVE
Serve with a mix of cubed and crushed ice in a large footed pilsner glass and garnish with a mint sprig.

STRENGTH SCALE

Shanghai Express

An original cocktail created by Kelly. In 1932, the eponymous film that inspired this cocktail was released. It was directed by Josef von Sternberg and starred Marlene Dietrich. The film was a massive hit in America. It remade twice as *Night Plane from Chungking* in 1942 and *Peking Express* in 1951. The original film was nominated for three Oscars, including best picture, best director and a win for best cinematography. This cocktail is a sure winner!

1 oz Regular Lemon Hart 151 Rum

1 oz Cruzan Light Rum

1 oz Chambord Raspberry Liqueur

2 oz Homemade Ginger Syrup

1 oz Freshly Squeezed Lime Juice

A splash of Soda Water

TO SERVE
Served in a cocktail glass with a raw sugar cane swizzle and a long strand of twisted lemon peel hanging over the edge.

STRENGTH SCALE

Shaka Hula Bossa Nova

South Seas Serenade

South Seas Serenade

A Tom cocktail that is guaranteed NOT to taste like your grandmother's lavender soap.

2 oz Rhum J.M. Martinique Rum

1½ oz Homemade Lavender Syrup

1½ oz Fresh Lemon Juice

1 oz Soda Water

TO SERVE
Add all liquids and shake with crushed ice, then garnish with a fresh purple orchid blossom.

STRENGTH SCALE

Stranded in Paradise

An original Kelly Hiphipahula creation that is completely influenced by island flavours. The name of the cocktail was inspired by the eponymous song title, written by Jim Bacchi, and performed by the Tikiyaki Orchestra. To be stranded on an island paradise may not be the worst thing ever to happen, especially if it's with a lover, at sunset and with a cocktail in hand.

2 oz Cruzan Mango Rum

1 oz Cruzan Light Rum

½ oz Chambord Raspberry Liqueur

½ oz Monin Watermelon Syrup

1½ oz Freshly Squeezed Lemon Juice

2–3 Lemon Wedges

TO SERVE
Shake with crushed ice and serve in a footed pilsner glass with an umbrella that has a cherry, pineapple, and a lime wedge balanced on the edge of the glass.

STRENGTH SCALE

Sultry Seductress

This is a Kelly original first served at La Descarga in Los Angeles, California, a well-known Cuban speakeasy rum and cigar bar. Not unlike the beautiful women of tiki and exotica music culture, this cocktail surrounds itself in a sexy aura. Slip into your smoking jacket or silky negligee, mix up a Sultry Seductress and let the sounds of Martin Denny's *Primitiva* seduce you.

2 oz Vizcaya VXOP Cask No. 21 Rum

1 oz Homemade Pimento Allspice Syrup

½ oz Cointreau Orange Liqueur

1 oz Dole Pineapple Juice

½ oz Orange Juice

½ oz Freshly Squeezed Lime Juice

TO SERVE
Flash blend all ingredients with crushed ice and serve in a footed pilsner. Garnish with a tall pineapple leaf.

STRENGTH SCALE

Sweet Antona

Sweet Antona was invented by Kelly. This drink features a delicious rum from the British West Indies, a secret blend of spices from French Carthusian monks, Italian pistachio liqueur, and fresh juice mixed with a float of funky Jamaican pot still to awaken your secret desires!

1 oz Dumante Pistachio Liqueur

1 oz Yellow Chartreuse

1 oz Angostura 1824 Rum

1 oz Freshly Squeezed Lemon Juice

½ oz Besamim Aromatic Spice Liqueur

½ oz Hamilton Pot Still Rum Float

TO SERVE
Shake with crushed ice all but the float, add the float, and then serve in a cognac snifter glass. Garnish with flower of lemon peel on a pick.

STRENGTH SCALE

Sweet Antona

Tahitian Twister

Tahitian Twister

This was invented by Tom at the Rumpus Room in La Crescenta, California. His friend, Eric October, had brought in some homemade sesame syrup for him to experiment with and this is what they came up with. Very tasty!

1 oz Homemade Sesame Syrup

1 oz Cruzan Coconut Rum

1½ oz Freshly Squeezed Lemon Juice

1 oz El Dorado 12-Year-Old Demerara Rum

1 oz Kern's Farm Mango Nectar

TO SERVE
Shake with crushed ice and serve in a lowball glass. Garnish with a slice of fresh mango speared through with a pitted cherry on either side.

STRENGTH SCALE

Tiki MojoHeato

Tired of muddling and getting flecks of mint stuck in your front teeth? Get your mojo on with this spicy and flavourful twist on the classic mojito! This drink was created by Kelly for Kari Hendler and her friends at Poly Hai in 2016. Founded in 2014, Poly Hai is a privately-funded online public high school for tikiphiles dedicated to the preservation and extension of the Polynesian pop lifestyle. Among other things, they are known for their annual class yearbook. You can see more about them on Facebook @polyhaischool.

2 oz Ron Diplomatico Blanco

⅔ oz Mint Syrup

½ oz Ancho Reyes Liqueur

1 oz Freshly Squeezed Lime Juice

TO SERVE
Build the cocktail in a collins glass filled with crushed ice and then transfer it to your shaker tin and shake vigorously. Return the contents to the glass and garnish with plenty of fresh mint sprigs. Add a cherry on a pick. As mint syrups vary in strength, alter the amount of syrup to suit your taste.

STRENGTH SCALE

Trader Tom's Rum Punch

Tom invented this at the Rumpus Room in La Crescenta, California. This punch is inspired by traditional red-coloured Jamaican rum punches, but instead of grenadine, this punch gets its lovely red colouring from blood orange syrup. Also, instead of the more common pineapple and orange juice mix blend, Tom uses the much heavier guava nectar. El Dorado is a premium touch and much more extravagant than the "well" rums used to make your typical Jamaican punch, but occasionally, you need to indulge yourself!

2 oz El Dorado 12-Year-Old Demerara Rum

1 oz Coruba Dark Jamaican Rum

½ oz Monin Blood Orange Syrup

3 oz Freshly Squeezed Lime Juice

1 oz Kern's Farm Guava Nectar

1 oz BG Reynolds Orgeat Almond Syrup

1 oz Soda Water

½ oz BG Reynolds Cinnamon Syrup

TO SERVE
Shake with crushed ice and garnish with a mint sprig Usually served in a two-sided tiki head glass..

STRENGTH SCALE

Trader Tom's Wayward Rum Barrel

Trader Tom has so many cocktail vessels that sometimes they get lost, drifting around in the turbulent waters of his tiki bar for quite some time until they are rediscovered and put to good use. Here is a recipe he came up with to re-baptise a prodigal rum barrel that went missing and then returned to the fold.

1 oz Panamá-Pacific 9 Year Rum

1 oz Appleton 12 Year Dark Jamaican

1 oz Ed Hamilton 151 Overproof Demerara

½ oz St. Elizabeth's Pimento Liqueur

¾ oz BG Reynolds Passionfruit Syrup

¾ oz Clover Honey Syrup Mix

1 oz Fresh Orange Juice

2 oz Fresh Lime Juice

3 shakes Angostura Bitters

3 drops Letherbee Charred Oak Absinthe

TO SERVE
Build this drink with crushed ice in a mixing tin and then swizzle it briefly using a Hamilton blender. Serve in your favourite rum barrel mug that will hold 12-16 oz.

STRENGTH SCALE

Trader Tom's Wayward Rum Barrel

Velvet Taboo

Two Black Eyes

Created by Kelly and named by Tom. Two guys come into a tiki bar, one of whom is wearing a fez. They order a cocktail and debate whether fezzes belong in Polynesian Pop culture. Before you know it a fight breaks out! Who won? Did two guys have one black eye, or did one guy have two black eyes? Moral of the story: when you have a cocktail with both blackstrap rum and black pepper syrup you end up with Two Black Eyes.

1 oz Cruzan Light Rum

¾ oz Cruzan Blackstrap Rum

¼ oz Yellow Chartreuse liqueur

½ oz Orange Curaçao liqueur

½ oz Homemade Black Pepper syrup

1 oz Homemade Sweet and Sour Syrup Mix

1 oz Freshly Squeezed Lime Juice

A splash of Soda Water

TO SERVE
Add all ingredients to tin with crushed ice, shake, and serve in a Tom Collins glass. Garnish on the side with two Luxardo dark cherries (black eyes) on a pick.

STRENGTH SCALE

Velvet Taboo

A cocktail by Kelly inspired by the velvet wahines of Edgar Leeteg and Ralph Burke Tyree whose nude forms graced the interiors of many a vintage tiki bar.

2½ oz Ron Zacapa 23 Solera Rum

½ oz Homemade Prickly Pear Syrup

½ oz Crème de Cassis Black Currant Liqueur

 1 dash (⅛ teaspoon) of St. Elizabeth's Pimento Allspice Liqueur

1 oz Freshly Squeezed Lemon Juice

A splash of Soda Water

TO SERVE
Shake with crushed ice and serve in a rocks/old fashioned glass with a lemon wheel floating on top.

STRENGTH SCALE

Vox Dei

Co-created by Tom & Kelly. *Vox Dei* is Latin and translates as "Voice of God". The complexity of the grassy Martinique rum and the caraway-flavoured Aquavit blends with the cardamom bitters and overproof rum, resulting in a whispered commandment that only you can hear!

1 oz Brennivan Aquavit

3/4 oz Rhum JM Gold

1/2 oz Hamilton 151 Overproof Demerara Rum

1 drop Scrappy's Cardamom Bitters

3/4 oz Simple Syrup

3/4 oz Freshly Squeezed Lime Juice

1/4 oz Monin Pomegranate Syrup

TO SERVE
Flash blend with crushed ice and strain into a chilled coupe glass. Garnish with a large Luxardo cherry on a pick.

STRENGTH SCALE

Volcano Cooler

This was invented by Tom at the Rumpus Room in La Crescenta, California. If you have a carton of POG (Pineapple/Orange juice/Guava), you may use that without having to measure out three different juices. This is a very refreshing red punch drink and proved very popular with the rumpusing crowd.

1 oz Cruzan White Rum

1 oz Coruba Dark Jamaican Rum

1 oz Kern's Farm Guava Nectar

2 oz Freshly Squeezed Lemon Juice

1 oz Smooth (no bits) Orange Juice

1 oz Unsweetened Pineapple Juice

A splash of Soda Water

1 oz Monin Blood Orange Syrup

1 oz BG Reynolds Orgeat Almond Syrup

TO SERVE
Shake with crushed ice and serve in your favourite tiki mug or a hurricane glass. Garnish with a paper umbrella with cherry, fresh pineapple wedge, and lemon wedge.

STRENGTH SCALE

Volcano Cooler

Waiting for Watubi

Waikiki Serenade

This is a Kelly original whose sweet sultry melody is sure to entrance your taste buds!

2 oz Cruzan Single Barrel Rum

1 oz Lemon Hart 80 Proof Rum

½ oz Orgeat Almond Syrup

2 oz Freshly Squeezed Lime Juice

¼ oz Pimento Allspice Dram

¼ oz St. Germain Elderflower Liqueur

¼ oz Homemade Lemongrass Syrup

¼ oz Torani Passionfruit Syrup

A splash of Soda Water

TO SERVE
Shake with crushed ice and serve in a Collins Glass or a tiki mug with an orchid flower or hibiscus garnish.

STRENGTH SCALE

Waiting for Watubi

Named after an episode of *Gilligan's Island*, Watubi is also a semi-legendary medicine man known throughout the South Pacific. Kelly delivers this witch doctor's tonic with a whale of a wallop. One, two, three, four, five rums with a primitive streak; including Jamaican and Navy Rums. Will send you screaming into the lagoon.

1 oz Smith & Cross Dark Jamaican Rum

1 oz Appleton 12 Year Dark Rum

1 oz Pusser's Dark Guyana Navy Rum

¼ oz Cruzan Blackstrap Rum

1 oz Homemade Black Pepper Syrup

½ oz Homemade Hibiscus Syrup

1 oz White Grapefruit Juice

½ oz Freshly Squeezed Lime Juice

A dash (⅛ teaspoon) of Angostura Bitters

A float ½ oz of Lemon Hart 151 Rum

TO SERVE
Shake with crushed ice and pour into a footed pilsner glass or a tiki mug. Add a spear swizzle stick.

STRENGTH SCALE

Winter Fling

Trader Tom created this drink. The fresh unpasteurised cider and pimento dram feels like Christmas, and baby, it's cold out there. Come in for a Winter Fling!

4 oz Fresh Apple Cider

1 oz Plantation Three Star White Rum

½ oz Remy Martin Cognac

¼ oz Pimento Dram

¼ oz Aperol

¼ oz Fresh Lemon Juice

TO SERVE
Shake with crushed ice and serve in a lowball glass. Garnish with an orange wheel on the side.

STRENGTH SCALE

Woohoo Wahine

This original libation was created by Kelly in honour of Woohoo Wahine (Karen Garland) who, with her husband, Chris Garland, run the Original Tiki Marketplace in Garden Grove, California. Kelly was behind the stick at the Tonga Hut in North Hollywood. Several people at the bar were organising an art show to be held there, and it was suggested by a friend that an original cocktail be created to entice tikiphiles living in Orange County to drop by. It is sometimes said that people who live in Orange County never leave it, coining the phrase, "Behind the Orange Curtain". So Kelly chose her good friend and Orange County resident, WooHoo Wahine, to promote the cocktail and, voila... it worked. They came in droves!

1 oz Cruzan Light Rum

1 oz Coruba Dark Jamaican Rum

¼ oz St Germain Liqueur

1 oz Homemade Hibiscus Syrup

2 oz Kern's Farm Guava Nectar

1½ oz Freshly Squeezed Lime Juice

A splash of Homemade Sweet and Sour Mix

A splash of Soda Water

A float of Cruzan Mango Rum

TO SERVE
Shake with crushed ice and pour into a footed pilsner with an umbrella spear garnish including a cherry, a pineapple chunk and a lime wedge.

STRENGTH SCALE

Winter Fling

Zombie Jamboree

The Wrecked Wench

This was created, by Kelly, for Jake Geiger's home bar, The Wrecked Wench. At his request, it is very similar to a Pele's Kiss, but without the ancho flavouring which is a time-consuming syrup to make. Even though Ancho Reyes Chili Liqueur is readily available these days, this cocktail still has a charm all of its own.

2 oz Cruzan Coconut Rum

1 oz Cruzan Vanilla Rum

¼ oz Bols Cherry Liqueur

1 oz Cracked Black Pepper Syrup

¼ oz Disaronno Almond Liqueur

1 oz Orange Juice

1 oz Freshly Squeezed Lime Juice

An optional Float of Lemon Hart 151 Rum

TO SERVE
Shake with crushed ice and serve in a pirate mug with cherries on a sword skewer.

STRENGTH SCALE

Zombie Jamboree

Tom created this cocktail, specifically, for the 2008 Tiki Oasis Drink Crawl.

5 oz Calamansi Lime Juice by Sun Tropics

4 oz Soursop/Guanabana Juice by Sun Tropics

3 oz Cruzan Light Rum

¼ oz Cocopandan Syrup

3¾ oz crushed ice

TO SERVE
Sun Tropics juices come in refrigerated cartons. The recipe makes 16 oz. Serve in a zombie head mug. Garnish with two Pitted Cherries on an umbrella with a lime wedge sandwiched between.

STRENGTH SCALE

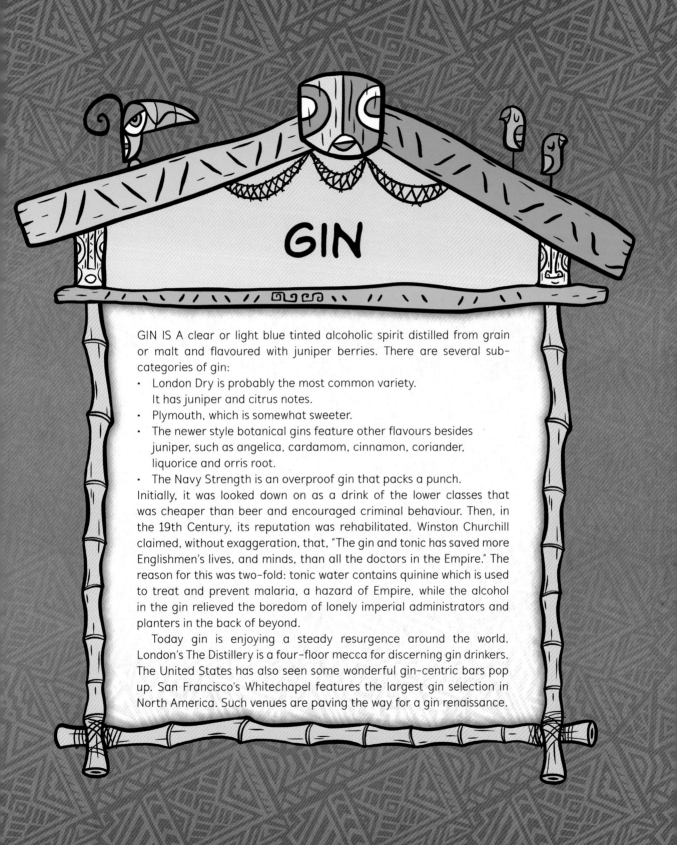

GIN

GIN IS A clear or light blue tinted alcoholic spirit distilled from grain or malt and flavoured with juniper berries. There are several sub-categories of gin:

- London Dry is probably the most common variety. It has juniper and citrus notes.
- Plymouth, which is somewhat sweeter.
- The newer style botanical gins feature other flavours besides juniper, such as angelica, cardamom, cinnamon, coriander, liquorice and orris root.
- The Navy Strength is an overproof gin that packs a punch.

Initially, it was looked down on as a drink of the lower classes that was cheaper than beer and encouraged criminal behaviour. Then, in the 19th Century, its reputation was rehabilitated. Winston Churchill claimed, without exaggeration, that, "The gin and tonic has saved more Englishmen's lives, and minds, than all the doctors in the Empire." The reason for this was two-fold: tonic water contains quinine which is used to treat and prevent malaria, a hazard of Empire, while the alcohol in the gin relieved the boredom of lonely imperial administrators and planters in the back of beyond.

Today gin is enjoying a steady resurgence around the world. London's The Distillery is a four-floor mecca for discerning gin drinkers. The United States has also seen some wonderful gin-centric bars pop up. San Francisco's Whitechapel features the largest gin selection in North America. Such venues are paving the way for a gin renaissance.

Bachelor Number One

This is a Kelly recipe based on the cocktail of choice of James Bond 007: The Vesper. The Vesper was originally made with Lillet Kina which is not available today. It is said that the Cocchi Americano is the closest to the bitter taste of the Kina. You may also want to experiment with bitters in lieu of Lillet or aperitifs. Kelly is a tiki wahini to the end and usually finds a way to add a little island flavour to your day, thus the PAMA.

4 oz Edinburgh Gin

½ oz Cocchi Americano (aperitif)
or Lillet Blanc if you prefer

½ oz PAMA Pomegranate Liqueur

TO SERVE
Measure all ingredients into a shaker tin with clean, filtered cubed ice and shake. Remember, "Shaken Not Stirred." Strain into a chilled martini glass or champagne coupe. Garnish with a lemon twist.

STRENGTH SCALE

Bamboo Splitter

This is a Tom creation that is light, minty, and refreshing without being overly sweet. Created during a break after using a draw knife to split bamboo for trim on a tiki project at the Hoodoo Hut 1.0: Tom's first version of his tiki room up in Portland.

1½ oz Schramm Botanical Gin

1 oz Honey Syrup

½ oz Yellow Chartreuse

1 oz White Grapefruit Juice

3 Muddled Mint Leaves

1 oz Freshly Squeezed Lemon Juice

TO SERVE
Shake with crushed ice and serve in a lowball glass with a grapefruit wheel on the side.

STRENGTH SCALE

Bamboo Splitter

The Eichler

Charlie Chan's Solution

Fu Manchu, the infamous supervillain with a moustache named after him, has carved out a niche in tiki culture with his popular mug, but there is as yet no mug for the Chinese detective Charlie Chan. Tom was inspired by Chan's 1948 film *The Feathered Serpent*, which despite being set in Aztec ruins, features a Tahitian style tiki prominently on the poster and in the film.

1½ oz Bombay Sapphire Gin

1½ oz Pineapple Juice

½ oz Freshly Squeezed Lemon Juice

½ oz BG Reynolds Passionfruit Syrup

¼ oz Aperol

TO SERVE
Shake with crushed ice and serve in a tiki mug. Garnish with a pineapple leaf and fresh pineapple wedge on a spear.

STRENGTH SCALE

The Eichler

Created by Kelly. Featuring Martin Miller's Gin bound by fruits of the garden, flowers on the vine and citrus off the tree. A crisp and refreshing bouquet.

Inspired by property developer Joseph Eichler, who built nearly 11,000 single-family homes in California, beginning in the late 1940s. Together these thousands of "Eichlers" reflect the beauty and uniqueness of the Eichler design and the integrity and daring of the builder behind it. With a modern look for the masses, these houses use open floor plans and whole walls of glass that blur the lines between indoor and outdoor spaces. With this cocktail, only a thin wall of glass separates you from a garden full of flavours. Enjoy!

2 oz Martin Miller's Gin

1 oz Homemade Rhubarb Syrup

½ oz Freshly Squeezed Lime Juice

½ oz St Germain's Elderflower Liqueur

2 drops Peychaud's Bitters

A splash of Soda Water

TO SERVE
Shake with crushed ice and serve in a double Old Fashioned glass with a stick of red rhubarb as a swizzle stick.

STRENGTH SCALE

Fu Manchu's Elixir Vitae

Tom invented this, looking for an exotic drink worthy of Fu Manchu. The Elixir Vitae is a magic potion that gives its imbiber added longevity. It explains Fu Manchu's long lifespan.

½ oz Remy Martin V.S.O.P. Cognac

1 oz Bombay Sapphire Gin

1 oz Freshly Squeezed Lemon Juice

1 oz Kronan Swedish Punsch

½ oz St. Germain's Elderflower Liqueur

1 oz BG Reynolds Orgeat Almond Syrup

TO SERVE
Serve in a Fu Manchu mug. Shake with crushed ice and serve with a pineapple leaf and a flower for garnish.

STRENGTH SCALE

Hakodate Hiball Modern

This was Kelly's creation for John-O's & the Ding Dong Devils' Mr Moto's International Club at Tiki Oasis 12. It was inspired by the hangover cure Hakodate Hiball in the film *Think Fast, Mr. Moto* (1937). In the film, the drink includes Worcestershire sauce, absinthe, a raw egg and plenty of gin. Kelly's modern twist, however, is a delicious cocktail with only the name in common.

Mr Moto is a fictional Japanese secret agent created by the author John P. Marquand. Between 1937 and 1939 eight motion pictures were produced starring the actor Peter Lorre as Mr Moto. Unlike in the novels, Moto is a detective with Interpol, wears glasses and has no gold teeth.

2 oz Bombay Sapphire Gin

A slight amount of Fresh Thyme

½ oz Homemade Hibiscus Syrup

½ oz Homemade Rhubarb Syrup

¼ oz Domaine de Canton Ginger Liqueur

¼ oz St. Germain Elderflower Liqueur

1¼ oz Freshly Squeezed Lime Juice

A splash of Soda Water

TO SERVE
Shake with crushed ice and serve in a footed pilsner glass. Garnish with two chopsticks as swizzles, an umbrella spear with a pineapple chunk, and a flower.

STRENGTH SCALE

Hakodate Hiball Modern

Lemon and Legerdemain

Lemons and Legerdemain

Tom invented this at his home bar in West Hills, California. Legerdemain is the skill of sleight of hand. The lemon interacts with the other ingredients to create some interesting tricks on the palate.

1½ oz Bombay Sapphire Gin

½ oz Navan Vanilla Liqueur, Tuaca, or Cruzan Vanilla

½ oz BG Reynolds' Passionfruit Syrup

1 drop Scrappy's Cardamom Bitters

1½ oz Freshly Squeezed Lemon Juice

TO SERVE
Add crushed ice to taste and serve in a lowball glass. Garnish with pineapple leaf and raw sugar cane swizzle stick.

STRENGTH SCALE

The Tattered Dress

Kelly was inspired by hardboiled detective novels of the 1940s and '50s, featuring damsels in distress with torn dresses. Careful, because some of those damsels turn out to be femme fatales!

1½ oz Citadel Gin

¾ oz Marie Brizard's Pear William Liqueur

½ oz Homemade Ginger Syrup

A splash of Club Soda

TO SERVE
Chill a cocktail glass and then shake the ingredients with ice in a tin and strain into the chilled glass. Rim the glass with two slices of peeled and squeezed mandarin fruit, then throw it in with the drink.

STRENGTH SCALE

The Vanguard

This cocktail was invented by Kelly, who says: "I wanted the feel of cool jazz to hard bop music playing in your head as you sip your way through this drink. It's 1962, we're all at the Village Vanguard in New York, listening to the greatest hipsters of all time... Feel it?... I'll take you there."

1 oz Caorunn Scottish Gin

1 oz Agwa Liqueur

½ oz Chambord Liqueur

½ oz Velvet Falernum

½ oz Simple Syrup

1 oz Freshly Squeezed Lime Juice

3-5 Mint Leaves

TO SERVE
In an Old Fashioned Glass (Rocks Glass). Muddle mint leaves and simple syrup. Then add crushed ice and the remaining ingredients. Return to the shaker tin and shake vigorously. Garnish with a mint sprig, a lime wedge and an optional raspberry.

STRENGTH SCALE

The Wright

In the spirit of Frank Lloyd Wight's combined love of architecture and agriculture, Kelly offers "The Wright." Frank Lloyd Wright grew up on the rolling hillsides of Wisconsin, where he enjoyed tending the grape vines and apple orchards, and looking after acres of fruits and vegetables. This love of nature eventually fed into his desire to design buildings that existed in harmony with their natural surroundings.

1 oz Botanist Gin

¾ oz Moletto Grappa

¼ oz Handmade Lavender Syrup

¼ oz Simple Syrup

A splash of Soda Water

TO SERVE
Muddle 4–6 green grapes in the tin with simple syrup. Build cocktail in a rocks glass with other ingredients and crushed ice, then pour back into the tin with the muddled grapes, shake, then strain into rocks glass. Add fresh ice. Garnish with fresh grapes on a pick.

STRENGTH SCALE

The Wright

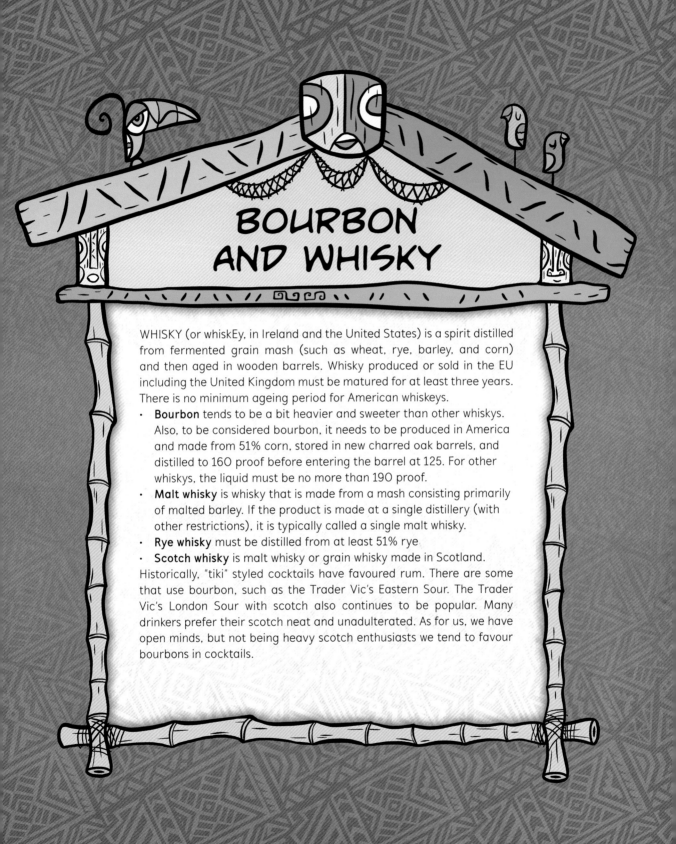

BOURBON AND WHISKY

WHISKY (or whiskEy, in Ireland and the United States) is a spirit distilled from fermented grain mash (such as wheat, rye, barley, and corn) and then aged in wooden barrels. Whisky produced or sold in the EU including the United Kingdom must be matured for at least three years. There is no minimum ageing period for American whiskeys.

- **Bourbon** tends to be a bit heavier and sweeter than other whiskys. Also, to be considered bourbon, it needs to be produced in America and made from 51% corn, stored in new charred oak barrels, and distilled to 160 proof before entering the barrel at 125. For other whiskys, the liquid must be no more than 190 proof.
- **Malt whisky** is whisky that is made from a mash consisting primarily of malted barley. If the product is made at a single distillery (with other restrictions), it is typically called a single malt whisky.
- **Rye whisky** must be distilled from at least 51% rye
- **Scotch whisky** is malt whisky or grain whisky made in Scotland.

Historically, "tiki" styled cocktails have favoured rum. There are some that use bourbon, such as the Trader Vic's Eastern Sour. The Trader Vic's London Sour with scotch also continues to be popular. Many drinkers prefer their scotch neat and unadulterated. As for us, we have open minds, but not being heavy scotch enthusiasts we tend to favour bourbons in cocktails.

Baron Samedi's Hoodoo Brew

This was invented by Tom. Baron Samedi is one of the most powerful of the Voodoo loa (spirits). As well as being master of the dead, Baron Samedi is also a giver of life. He can cure any mortal of any disease or wound, if he thinks it is worthwhile. His powers are especially great when it comes to Voodoo curses and black magic. Even if somebody has been afflicted by a hex which brings them to the verge of death, they will not die if the Baron refuses to dig their grave. So long as this mighty spirit keeps them out of the ground, they are safe. This brew is guaranteed to bring life back to any party!

2 oz Woodford Reserve Bourbon

½ oz John D. Taylor's Velvet Falernum

¼ oz BG Reynold's Passionfruit Syrup

1 oz Freshly Squeezed Lemon Juice.

½ oz Domaine de Canton Ginger Liqueur

¼ oz Club Soda

TO SERVE
Shake with crushed ice and garnish with Orange Wedge. Serve in a lowball glass.

STRENGTH SCALE

Bokor's Bastard

This was invented by Tom. This is a riff on the classic Suffering Bastard cocktail. Bokors are Voodoo witch doctors for hire who are said to serve the loa (spirits) with both hands, meaning that they practice both dark magic and light magic. This cocktail blends both gin and bourbon, strong and weak, sweet and sour, for a cocktail that lives life on the edge.

1½ oz Woodford Reserve Bourbon

1 oz Hendrick's Gin

1 dash of Angostura Bitters

¼ oz Senior's Brand Curaçao

1 oz Freshly Squeezed Lime Juice

3 oz Strong Ginger Beer

1 oz Clover Honey Syrup

TO SERVE
Shake with crushed ice and garnish with a cucumber spear. Serve in a lowball glass.

SSTRENGTH SCALE

Baron Samedi's Hoodoo Brew

Holy Molé

Holy Molé

This was invented by Tom and Kelly. It's a playful tribute to the popular Mexican dish, Mole Poblano.

1 oz Woodford Reserve Bourbon

½ oz Kaluha Coffee Liqueur

½ oz Orgeat Almond Syrup

3 shakes Fee Brothers Aztec Chocolate Bitters

1 oz Freshly Squeezed Lemon Juice

TO SERVE
Add crushed ice to taste and serve in a lowball glass. Garnish with a pineapple leaf and a length of curled lemon peel.

STRENGTH SCALE

Lola O'Brien

This was invented by Kelly and was inspired by the famous song, "Lola O'Brien the Irish Hawaiian" by Lawrence Welk.

1½ oz Jameson's Irish Whiskey

¼ oz Drambuie

¾ oz Homemade Hibiscus Syrup

1 oz Orange Juice

A splash of Soda Water

A shake of Orange Bitters

TO SERVE
Add crushed ice in an Old Fashioned glass, add the above ingredients and then move ingredients to a tin, shake, and serve in the Old Fashioned glass.

STRENGTH SCALE

The Marked Man

The mark of Cain? The mark of Zorro? Marked for Death? Or, marked for Glory? However you make your mark, raise a toast with this cocktail of Kelly's whose rich bourbon flavour and spicy notes are just what a marked man needs.

1 oz Maker's Mark 46 Kentucky Bourbon

1 oz Licor 43

¾ oz Homemade Pepper Syrup

½ oz Freshly Squeezed Lime Juice

TO SERVE
Add crushed ice in an Old Fashioned glass, add the above ingredients and then move the ingredients to a tin, shake, and serve in the Old Fashioned glass.

STRENGTH SCALE

Rathbone's Deduction

Created by Tom & Kelly in honour of Basil Rathbone, one of the original actors who played Sir Arthur Conan Doyle's Sherlock Holmes on film.

1 oz Woodford Reserve Bourbon

½ oz Orgeat Almond Syrup

½ oz PAMA Pomegranate Liqueur

1 oz Freshly Squeezed Lime Juice

1 muddled Basil Leaf

TO SERVE
Muddle the basil leaf and then add crushed ice in an Old Fashioned glass, add the above ingredients and then move ingredients to a tin, shake, and serve in the Old Fashioned glass.

STRENGTH SCALE

Rathbone's Deduction

Slipping the Great Beyond

The Sleep of Reason

This was invented by Tom & Kelly in November 2015, and was inspired by the etching *The Sleep of Reason Produces Monsters*, by the Spanish painter and printmaker Francisco Goya (1746-1828).

1 oz Woodford Reserve Bourbon

½ oz Solerno Blood Orange Liqueur

½ oz Ancho Reyes Liqueur

½ oz Freshly Squeezed Lemon Juice

½ oz Homemade Cinnamon Syrup

TO SERVE
Add crushed ice to taste and serve in a lowball glass. Garnish with a blood orange wheel on the rim.

STRENGTH SCALE

Slipping the Great Beyond

This drink is one of Tom's creations. It is simply sublime. The rye handles these strong fruit flavours, and the pimento spice takes it over the edge. "Indeed it is possible to stand with one foot on the inevitable 'banana peel' of life with both eyes peering into the Great Beyond, and still be happy, comfortable, and serene — if we will even so much as smile." — Douglas Fairbanks

1 oz Templeton Rye Whiskey

½ oz 99 Bananas Liqueur

1 oz Pineapple Juice

½ oz Homemade Pimento Allspice Syrup

1 oz Freshly Squeezed Lemon Juice

TO SERVE
Shake with crushed ice and serve in a lowball glass. Garnish with a pineapple leaf and spear with fresh pineapple chunk on the rim.

STRENGTH SCALE

Taboo Tsantsa

This was invented by Tom in 2012. Inspired by the Tropical Itch cocktail with its blend of passionfruit, rum and bourbon, but with some fundamental changes. The original Tropical Itch cocktail was invented at the Hilton Hawaiian Village in Waikiki, Hawaii in 1957 by Harry Yee.

A *tsantsa* is a shrunken head, and too many of these cocktails will without question, shrink yours if you're not careful. It was served as a 3½-gallon pre-mix at Kirby's Rumpus Room in August 2017, for a celebrated re-opening after it had been shut for a few years.

1 oz Woodford Reserve Bourbon

1 oz Smith & Cross Jamaican Rum

1 oz Appleton Estate Jamaican Rum

½ oz Senior Brand Orange Curaçao

1 oz BG Reynolds Passionfruit Syrup

1 oz Freshly Squeezed Lemon Juice

1 oz Club Soda

3 drops Pernod

TO SERVE
Shake with crushed ice, serve in a lowball glass, and garnish with pitted cherries and an orange slice on spear.

STRENGTH SCALE

Tiki Templeton

This was invented by Tom and Kelly in November 2015. It features Templeton Rye Whiskey but with some exotic flavours that are sure to enliven any tiki temple! Templeton Rye was said to be the mobster Al Capone's drink of choice.

1¾ oz Templeton Rye Whiskey

1 oz Fresh Orange Juice

¼ oz St. Elizabeth's Pimento Allspice Dram

2 drops Fee Brothers Chocolate Aztec Bitters

½ oz Simple Syrup

TO SERVE
Add crushed ice, strain and serve in a chilled coupe glass. Garnish with a large mint leaf on top.

STRENGTH SCALE

Taboo Tsantsa

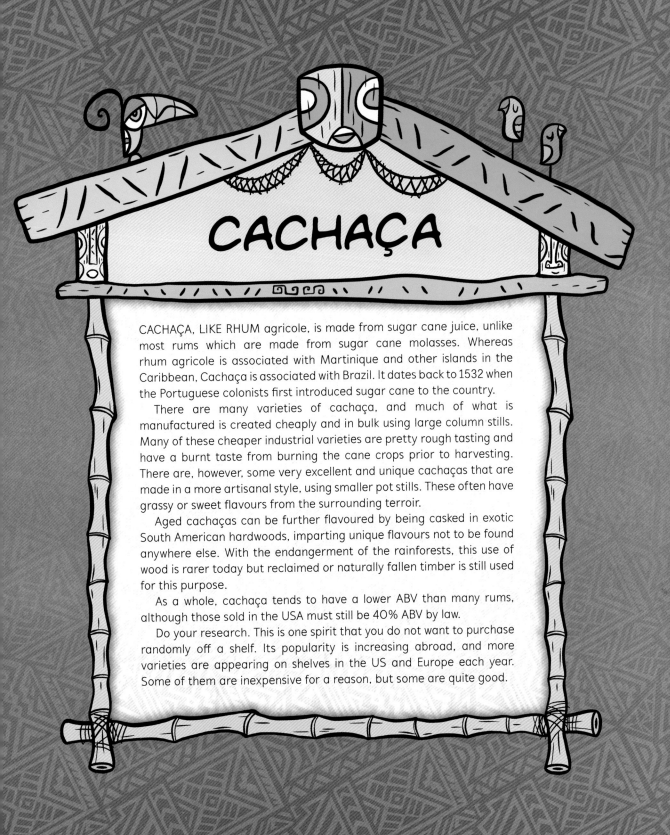

CACHAÇA

CACHAÇA, LIKE RHUM agricole, is made from sugar cane juice, unlike most rums which are made from sugar cane molasses. Whereas rhum agricole is associated with Martinique and other islands in the Caribbean, Cachaça is associated with Brazil. It dates back to 1532 when the Portuguese colonists first introduced sugar cane to the country.

There are many varieties of cachaça, and much of what is manufactured is created cheaply and in bulk using large column stills. Many of these cheaper industrial varieties are pretty rough tasting and have a burnt taste from burning the cane crops prior to harvesting. There are, however, some very excellent and unique cachaças that are made in a more artisanal style, using smaller pot stills. These often have grassy or sweet flavours from the surrounding terroir.

Aged cachaças can be further flavoured by being casked in exotic South American hardwoods, imparting unique flavours not to be found anywhere else. With the endangerment of the rainforests, this use of wood is rarer today but reclaimed or naturally fallen timber is still used for this purpose.

As a whole, cachaça tends to have a lower ABV than many rums, although those sold in the USA must still be 40% ABV by law.

Do your research. This is one spirit that you do not want to purchase randomly off a shelf. Its popularity is increasing abroad, and more varieties are appearing on shelves in the US and Europe each year. Some of them are inexpensive for a reason, but some are quite good.

Brazilian Buzz

It's a carnival in a glass! Try this cocktail by Kelly, and you'll be doing the bossa nova to Rio in double time! It was created at Jake Geiger's Wrecked Wench home bar in Winnetka, California.

2 oz Novo Fogo Barrel-aged Cachaça

2 oz Freshly Squeezed Lemon Juice

½ oz Agave Honey

1¼ oz Homemade Black Pepper Syrup

1 oz Kern's Farm Guava Nectar

TO SERVE
Prepare in a collins glass full of crushed ice, add all ingredients, pour into a shaker tin and shake vigorously. Return the cocktail to the collins glass. Garnish with a lemon wheel and a festive swizzle stick.

STRENGTH SCALE

Flaming Headless Mule

This was invented by Tom and Kelly in November 2015. The Headless Mule (Portuguese: mula sem cabeça) is a character in Brazilian folklore. In most tales, it is the ghost of a woman that has been condemned by God to turn into a fire-spewing headless mule from Thursday's sundown to Friday's sunrise for her sin of fornicating with a priest in Church. So...drink with caution.

1 oz Avuá Prata Cachaça

½ oz Homemade Ginger Syrup

1 squeezed Wedge of Lime

TO SERVE
Shake with crushed ice and pour into a footed pilsner glass. Then, add ginger beer almost to the top. Add an oz of overproof Lemon Hart 151 and top with a sugar cube soaked in the same. Light on fire!

STRENGTH SCALE

Flaming Headless Mule

Samba de Ipanema

Samba de Ipanema

A Kelly original. Take silver cachaça imported from Brazil and throw in Carmen Miranda and that sums it all up.

1½ oz Avuá Prata Cachaça

1 oz Veev Acai Liqueur

¾ oz Kern's Mango Nectar

½ oz BG Reynolds Passionfruit Syrup

A splash of Soda Water

TO SERVE
Muddle a small lime wedge with one sugar cube in the bottom of a tin shaker, then add the other components and shake with crushed ice before pouring into a collins glass. Add a splash of soda water and garnish with brightly coloured ribbons and straws.

STRENGTH SCALE

Tiki Batida

One of Kelly's favourite variations on a classic. In Brazil, *batida* means to shake or to blend with ice until smooth. This one is not shaken, however, which is a little ironic. This drink separates out into brightly coloured layers of unique liqueurs and nectars. A carnival in a glass!

2 oz Avuá Prata Cachaça

1 oz of Green Pistachio Syrup (Monin if available)

1 oz Freshly Squeezed Lemon Juice

½ oz Agave Honey Syrup (Medium)

¼ oz Homemade Ancho Pepper Syrup

1 oz Kern's Farm Guava Nectar

1 oz Kern's Farm Mango Nectar

3 shakes of Angostura Bitters

TO SERVE
You must float in order each of these ingredients within a hurricane glass. Garnish with ribbons and make sure not to break the delicate layers. Once served, the recipient should blend the ingredients with their straw or swizzle.

STRENGTH SCALE

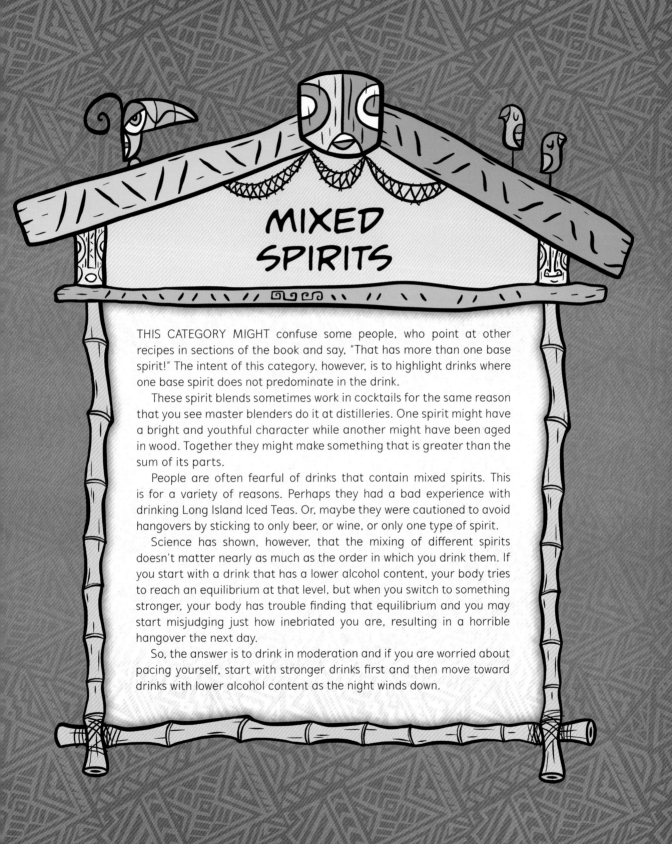

MIXED SPIRITS

THIS CATEGORY MIGHT confuse some people, who point at other recipes in sections of the book and say, "That has more than one base spirit!" The intent of this category, however, is to highlight drinks where one base spirit does not predominate in the drink.

These spirit blends sometimes work in cocktails for the same reason that you see master blenders do it at distilleries. One spirit might have a bright and youthful character while another might have been aged in wood. Together they might make something that is greater than the sum of its parts.

People are often fearful of drinks that contain mixed spirits. This is for a variety of reasons. Perhaps they had a bad experience with drinking Long Island Iced Teas. Or, maybe they were cautioned to avoid hangovers by sticking to only beer, or wine, or only one type of spirit.

Science has shown, however, that the mixing of different spirits doesn't matter nearly as much as the order in which you drink them. If you start with a drink that has a lower alcohol content, your body tries to reach an equilibrium at that level, but when you switch to something stronger, your body has trouble finding that equilibrium and you may start misjudging just how inebriated you are, resulting in a horrible hangover the next day.

So, the answer is to drink in moderation and if you are worried about pacing yourself, start with stronger drinks first and then move toward drinks with lower alcohol content as the night winds down.

Dragon Junk

As exotic as sailing the China high seas! A cocktail created by Kelly Hiphipahula. Junks have been sailing the seas for centuries and are still in use today for fishing and trade in the coastal waters and rivers of China, Japan, and Indonesia. In Hong Kong harbour dinner and cocktail cruises are available to all, but you can just as easily mix up a Dragon Junk cocktail and enjoy it right here in your armchair and feel as if you were already there! Happy Sailing!

2 oz Freshly Squeezed Lemon Juice

1 oz Orange Juice

½ oz Disarrono Amaretto Liqueur

½ oz Hennessey Brandy

½ oz Botanist Islay Dry Gin or Bombay Sapphire

1½ oz Clement V.S.O.P. or Cruzan Light Rum

A special Liqueur Syrup Foam Float

A sprinkle of ground Cardamom, Cinnamon, Allspice, Anise, and Nutmeg

TO SERVE
Shake with crushed ice and serve in a footed pilsner glass and then add the special float and sprinkle.

Special Liqueur Syrup Foam Float consists of Kelly's Special Summer Port Reduction (see page 243) and heavy whipped cream. You may use milk for lighter consistency. The Special Summer Port Reduction is listed in the appendix. Garnish with mint sprigs and a large orange wheel on side.

STRENGTH SCALE

Erzuli's Love Punch

Tom created this cocktail. This is a more complicated version of a Peach Bellini with slightly more tartness and added herbal and floral notes. A nice variation for those significant others who want to visit a tiki bar but are put off by strong rum concoctions.

2 oz Kern's Farm Peach Nectar

½ oz St. Germain Elderflower Liqueur

2 oz Champagne

1 oz Freshly Squeezed Lemon Juice

½ oz Yellow Chartreuse

TO SERVE
Shake with crushed ice and then strain and serve in a champagne flute.

STRENGTH SCALE

Dragon Junk

The Krisel

French Whore's Boudoir

This cocktail was created in 2009 by both Tom and Kelly as a challenge to use all French (or in the case of the St. James rum, French-owned) ingredients. There are already many "French Whore" cocktails in existence that typically include vodka, Chambord, and pineapple juice. But we think such drinks are a little on common side, whereas this little lady is distinctly high class. Careful you don't get hooked!

1 oz St James Martinique Royal Amber Rum

1 oz Remy Martin Cognac

¼ oz St Germain's Elderflower Liqueur

½ oz Rock Candy Syrup

1 oz Ginger Ale

1 oz Freshly Squeezed Lemon Juice

1 oz Freshly Squeezed Lime Juice

TO SERVE
Shake with crushed ice and serve in a stemmed coupe glass. Garnish with a paper umbrella with three cherries on the side and a flower at the centre.

STRENGTH SCALE

The Krisel

A Kelly original. Very exotic, dry, light and smooth to the palate. Inspired by William Krisel, the architect, whose mid-century modern homes are still being enjoyed across California. Krisel is one of the few mid-century modern architects who has not only lived to see but also participated in the resurgence of modernism in Palm Springs. In recent years, he has contributed to the restoration of many of his original designs. Kelly grew up in Granada Hills, California, a neighbourhood populated by his homes.

2 oz Cana Brava Light Rum

1 oz Aviation Gin

¾ oz Home Made Lavender Syrup

1 oz Orange Juice

1 drop Peychaud's Orange Bitters

¼ Amaretto Almond Liqueur

¼ Liqor 43

1 oz Rhum Barbancourt 5 Star Rum

TO SERVE
Shake with crushed ice and strain into a large martini glass. Garnish with an orange twist.

STRENGTH SCALE

La Serena

"Serena" may mean "peaceful", but don't be fooled. This Kelly original is a dynamic, divine libation that is capable of wreaking havoc! She slips down easily and will beckon you back for more. But sailor beware: partake of just one then hoist your sail for home.

2 oz Rhum J.M.

2 oz Milagro Select Barrel Reserve Reposado Tequila

½ oz Freshly Squeezed Lemon Juice

½ oz Freshly Squeezed Lime Juice

2½ oz Home Made Tamarind Syrup

A float of Appleton 12 Year Jamaican Rum

A splash of Soda Water

TO SERVE
Shake with crushed ice and serve in your favourite mermaid mug.

STRENGTH SCALE

Makaha

Created by Kelly, *makaha* is Hawaiian for "fierce" or "savage." And that's precisely how you'll feel after imbibing one of these. The clear spirits blend with the creamy Amarula and other exotic flavours for a sweet sensation that packs a knockout punch!

1 oz Absolute vodka

1 oz Bombay Blue Sapphire gin

½ oz Galliano

½ oz Amarula liqueur

½ oz Blue Curaçao liqueur

1 oz Sweet and Sour

A float Homemade Hibiscus syrup

TO SERVE
Shake with crushed ice and serve in a footed pilsner glass. Garnish with an umbrella pick on the rim that has cherry, pineapple, and lime on it.

STRENGTH SCALE

La Serena

Peruvian Songbird

Oscalypso

A Kelly original for the hip cats and kittens who like to listen to smooth jazz and mellow out. Inspired by the music of Oscar Pettiford, one of the most-recorded bass-playing bandleader/composers in jazz.

2 oz Martinelli's Sparkling Cran-Apple Juice

½ oz Buffalo Trace Whiskey

½ oz Kōloa Kaua`i Spice Rum

¼ oz St. Germain Elderflower Liqueur

A splash of Soda Water

TO SERVE
Stir with ice cubes and strain into a coupe glass with a long cinnamon stick as a swizzle.

STRENGTH SCALE

Peruvian Songbird

Created by Trader Tom and inspired by Yma Sumac, a Peruvian-American soprano. In the 1950s, she was one of the most famous proponents of exotica music. Sumac became an international success based on her extreme vocal range, which was said to be well over five octaves at the peak of her singing career.

1 oz Plantation 3 Star White Rum

2 oz Capel Pisco

½ oz St. Germain's Elderflower Liqueur

1 oz Dole Pineapple Juice

1 oz Freshly Squeezed Lime Juice

½ oz Orgeat Almond Syrup

TO SERVE
Shake with crushed ice and serve in a rocks/old fashioned glass. Garnish with a pineapple leaf and pineapple spear.

STRENGTH SCALE

Satin Pearl

Tom and Kelly both designed this drink. The grassy notes of the agricole work well with the lush sesame and clean lemon flavours.

1 oz Rhum JM Agricole Gold

1 oz Absolut Mandarin Vodka

1 oz Homemade Sesame Syrup

1 oz Freshly Squeezed Lemon Juice

TO SERVE
Shake with crushed ice and serve in a hiball glass or vintage Pearl Diver glass. Lay a chopstick across the top with long lemon twist wrapped around it for garnish.

STRENGTH SCALE

Scorpion Prohibido

A Kelly cocktail inspired by the classic Scorpion Bowl, this single serving drink trades out gin for genever and substitutes a dark Jamaican rum for the more common Puerto Rican Gold Rum. Instead of lemon Kelly has added pimento syrup and lime. Different but familiar and very delicious. The Scorpion Prohibido (Forbidden Scorpion) has a bit of a sting but goes down smooth. For our bowl version see page 230.

1 oz Smith & Cross Jamaican Rum

1 oz Bols Genever

½ oz Homemade Pimento Syrup

¾ oz Christian Brothers Brandy

½ oz Orgeat Almond Syrup

1 oz Torani Passionfruit Syrup

1 oz Orange Juice

¾ oz Freshly Squeezed Lime Juice

TO SERVE
Shake with crushed ice and serve in a footed pilsner glass. Garnish with orange peel.

STRENGTH SCALE

Satin Pearl

Singapore Swing

Screaming Lorita

Created by Kelly, but who is Lorita and why is she screaming? Lorita is a noisy Spanish-speaking parrot but not just anyone's parrot. When the adventurer Thor Heyerdahl left the harbour at Callao, Peru, on April 28, 1947, the sixth member of his crew on the boat Kon-Tiki was Lorita.

½ oz Appleton v/x Rum

2 oz Kettle One Vodka

1 oz Remy Martin Cognac

¼ oz Galliano

¼ oz Maraschino Cherry Syrup

1 oz Freshly Squeezed Lemon Juice

1½ oz Soda Water

TO SERVE

Shake with crushed ice and serve in a colada or hurricane glass. Garnish with mint sprigs, a speared cherry and a twist of lemon.

STRENGTH SCALE

Singapore Swing

Created by Kelly, this is a riff on the Singapore Sling cocktail, that was developed by Ngiam Tong Boon at the Raffles Hotel sometime before 1915. This cocktail was inspired by the song of the same name, written by Jim Bacchi of the Tikiyaki Orchestra.

1 oz London Dry Gin

1 oz Plantation Three Star Light Rum

1 oz Bénédictine & Brandy (B&B)

1 oz Freshly Squeezed Lemon Juice

1 oz Cherry Brandy

1 oz Ginger Beer

½ oz Soda Water

TO SERVE

Shake with crushed ice and serve in a colada or hurricane glass. Garnish with mint sprigs and a speared cherry with a twist of lemon.

STRENGTH SCALE

TEQUILA AND MEZCAL

TEQUILA IS TECHNICALLY a mezcal. Tequila, however, is made using only the blue agave and can only be produced in the state of Jalisco in Mexico and small parts of four other states in the country.

Blue agave tequila is generally considered to be a superior product. There are, however, some very interesting mezcals on the market (from dozens of other varieties of the agave plant) with unique flavour profiles that work well in certain cocktails. Some mezcals have a very interesting smoke flavour that you will not find in regular blue agave tequila. This is because mezcal is typically produced by baking the hearts of the agave, or *pinas*, in earthen pits, which imparts a smoky flavour. As with other spirits, there are distilling, ageing and barreling factors to consider as well.

Overall, tequila production has boomed in recent years and is no longer just a cheap shooter for wild college parties. Just because a bottle of tequila is expensive, however, does not mean that it is the best value. Prices fluctuate because of other factors. Recent discussion has pointed out, not for the first time, that blue agave farming follows an 8–10 year-long cycle and as it nears the end of that cycle, mature plants become rarer, and the price spikes. As with rum and cachaça, you need to do your homework, but there is bound to be a label out there to suit every palate.

Aztec Hotel

The mezcal used in this cocktail is a blend of Salmiana, Americana and Epadin Agave from Tamaulipas. These wild agaves are cooked using mesquite wood, distilled twice, and then aged one year in used American oak barrels. Created by Trader Tom, this drink is a smoky chocolate citrus flavour with a hint of ginger.

Inspired by the architecture of the Aztec Hotel in Monrovia, California, which was designed by architect Robert Stacy-Judd, and built on the legendary original U.S. Route 66 in 1924.

1½ oz El Tinieblo Mezcal Anejo

1 oz Homemade Tamarind Syrup

2 shakes Aztec Chocolate Bitters

1 oz Freshly Squeezed lime juice

1 oz Pineapple Juice

1 oz Ginger Beer

½ oz Domaine de Canton Ginger Liqueur

TO SERVE
Shake with crushed ice and serve in an Aztec styled mug.

STRENGTH SCALE

Aztec Sacrifice

Just as with The Aztec Hotel, the mezcal used in this cocktail is a blend of Salmiana, Americana and Epadin Agave from Tamaulipas. These wild agaves are cooked using mesquite wood, distilled twice, and then aged one year in used American oak barrels. Created by Trader Tom, this drink is a smoky mango/passionfruit blend with just a touch of ancho pepper heat. Before imbibing, spill a few drops onto the ground as an offering to Mayahuel, the Aztec goddess of maguey (agave).

1½ oz El Tinieblo Mezcal Anejo

1 oz Kern's Farm Mango Nectar

1 oz Freshly Squeezed Lemon Juice

¼ oz Solerno Blood Orange Liqueur

¼ oz Ancho Reyes Liqueur

¼ oz BG Reynolds Passionfruit Syrup

TO SERVE
Shake with crushed ice and serve in an Aztec styled mug.

STRENGTH SCALE

Aztec Hotel

Cocktail Corrido

Aztec Treasure

The mezcal used in this cocktail is a blend of Salmiana, Americana and Epadin Agave from Tamaulipas. These wild agaves are cooked using mesquite wood, distilled twice, and then aged one year in used American oak barrels. Created by Trader Tom, the smoky mezcal in this cocktail plays with the honey syrup and hibiscus flavours and is balanced by the citrus juice and Hum's kaffir lime spice.

1 oz El Tinieblo Mezcal Anejo

¼ oz Hum Liqueur

1 oz Freshly Squeezed Lime Juice

1½ oz Homemade Honey Syrup

A splash of Club Soda

TO SERVE
Shake with crushed ice and serve in a rocks/old fashioned glass. Garnish with a wedge of orange on the side.

STRENGTH SCALE

Cocktail Corrido

A *corrido* is a popular narrative song and poetry form, a bit like a ballad. The songs are often about oppression, history, daily life, and other socially relevant topics. It is still a popular form today in Mexico. Kelly created this Corrido with Don the Beachcomber in mind, who often called his cocktails "Rum Rhapsodies." This is a tequila cocktail that will definitely give you something to sing about.

1½ oz Casamigos Blanco Blue Agave Tequila

1 rounded tbps of Kozlowski Five Pepper Preserves

2 pinches of Fresh Cilantro

½ oz Freshly Squeezed Lime Juice

TO SERVE
Mix the tablespoon of preserves with lime juice and set it aside to dissolve. Later, in a tin, muddle the melted preserves, lime, and cilantro. Build crushed ice in a collins glass with tequila, then empty into the tin, shake, and return to a salt-rimmed Collins glass.

STRENGTH SCALE

Flor de Jamaica

Created by Kelly and first served at the Tonga Hut, North Hollywood. Rose tequila and fresh in-house crafted Jamaica flower simple syrup set a floral mood, taste and feel you have never experienced.

1 oz Rose Tequila Asombroso

½ oz Grand Marnier

½ oz Freshly Squeezed Lemon Juice

½ oz Freshly Squeezed Lime Juice

1 oz Homemade Hibiscus (Jamaica) Syrup

1 oz St. Germain Elderflower Liqueur

½ oz St. Elizabeth's Spiced Dram or other pimento liqueur

A splash of Club Soda

TO SERVE

Chill the glass in advance. Serve in a Burgundy wine glass or just a large wine glass. Prepare the cocktail in a tin using 4 oz of small cubed ice. Rim the chilled glass with fine sugar. Pour the contents of the tin into your glassware without splashing the liquid on the sugar rim. Garnish with a hibiscus flower and cactus leaf. Syrup recipe on page 240 .

STRENGTH SCALE

Old Prickly

This is Trader Tom's favourite margarita drink. Tom first began experimenting with prickly pear syrup after a family trip to Sedona, Arizona. In addition to its natural beauty, Sedona is known for its shops, especially those featuring native arts and jewelry. Every third shop seemed to have some kind of prickly pear product featured, regardless of their other wares, and finally curiosity got the best of him. Since then, he's enjoyed having prickly pear in his cocktail arsenal to employ time and again as a surprising and refreshing flavour addition. Check out page 241 in the appendix to see how you can make your own homemade prickly pear syrup. The smokiness of the anejo tequila goes well with the prickly pear. This is a case where using a sipping tequila to mix with isn't blasphemy at all. It's a south of the border treat!

3 oz Tres Generaciones Anejo Tequila

½ oz Senior's Orange Curaçao

2 oz Homemade Prickly Pear Syrup

1½ oz Freshly Squeezed Lime Juice

TO SERVE

Serve in a margarita glass with a lightly salted rim with a lime wedge on the rim.

STRENGTH SCALE

Flor de Jamaica

Ricky Ricardo's Mistake

Ponch's Ponche

This is Tom's take on a traditional ponche. This recipe shows an individual serving size, but traditionally this is made in large batches and served hot throughout the evening. With its roots in the traditional Mexican Christmas punch, this is exactly what you would expect Eric Estrada's character, Frank "Ponch" Poncherello, to kick back with after a hard day at the job, busting bad guys with the other officers of California Highway Patrol, in the classic television show *CHiPs*. See page 230 in the chapter "Bowl Drinks" for the full party size version.

½ oz Tres Generaciones Anejo Tequila

1 oz Remy Martin Cognac

¼ oz Nocello Walnut Liqueur

¼ oz Hum Hibiscus Liqueur

2 drops Pernod

¼ oz Homemade or BG Reynolds Cinnamon Syrup

½ oz Freshly Squeezed Lemon Juice

1¾ oz Fresh Apple Cider

TO SERVE
Served hot in a coffee mug with an apple slice as garnish.

STRENGTH SCALE

Ricky Ricardo's Mistake

Lucy and Ricky Ricardo are a fictional comedy duo from the American television sitcom *I Love Lucy*. Ricky is a strait-laced Cuban-American bandleader. Lucy is his fiery red-headed wife who is always getting into mischief and trying to hide it from her husband. When caught, Ricky always says in his Cuban accent that she has "some 'splaining to do." Ricky's mistake was not warning Lucy that he preferred Cuban rum to tequila, but after she mixed this for him, He decided that maybe she was on to something after all. A Kelly original. Don't drink too many of these or you too might find yourself 'splaining!

2½ oz Don Julio Blanco Tequila

3 oz Freshly Squeezed Lime Juice

3 oz Homemade Ancho Chili Syrup

A splash of Soda Water

TO SERVE
Shake with crushed ice and serve in a pilsner glass.

STRENGTH SCALE

Sideshow Gaff

A sideshow gaff is a prop that is constructed to fool the public, such as the notorious Fiji mermaid made out of taxidermied parts from a fish and a monkey. P.T. Barnum exhibited the original Fiji mermaid in Barnum's American Museum in New York in 1842, after which it mysteriously disappeared. Tequila is generally not a favourite with the tiki crowd, who prefer rum. This is not, however, your typical tequila drink. The smoothness of the passionfruit and the unexpected bitterness of the Aperol give it an added complexity. Tom invented this cocktail.

1½ oz Milagro Silver Tequila

½ oz PAMA Pomegranate Liqueur

1 oz BG Reynolds Passionfruit Syrup

1 oz Freshly Squeezed Lime Juice

½ oz Aperol

TO SERVE
Build in a lowball glass and add crushed ice, then transfer to a shaker tin, shake, and return to the glass. Garnish with an orange wedge.

STRENGTH SCALE

Tah Quee Toe

A lively creation by Kelly. Tah Quee Toe gives you a fiery take on the classic Mojito but *más bien!* This cocktail premiered at Lush Goes Latin at the Tonga Hut in North Hollywood, California starring Marty Lush and His Latin Livers band. For the evening, Marty took on the persona of a 1950s-60s band leader. All of Marty's personas are lushes (alcoholics) however, this leads to some rather off-colour jokes much like Dean Martin's act. Marty even wore a Matador costume for the show. TORO!

2 oz Cazadores tequila

2 oz Homemade Black Pepper syrup

2 oz Freshly Squeezed Lime Juice

2 Lime Wedges

3 Large Mint Leaves

TO SERVE
Muddle the mint, syrup, and lime wedges in a lowball glass, then add other ingredients, including crushed ice. Then flash blend and serve.

STRENGTH SCALE

Tah Quee Toe

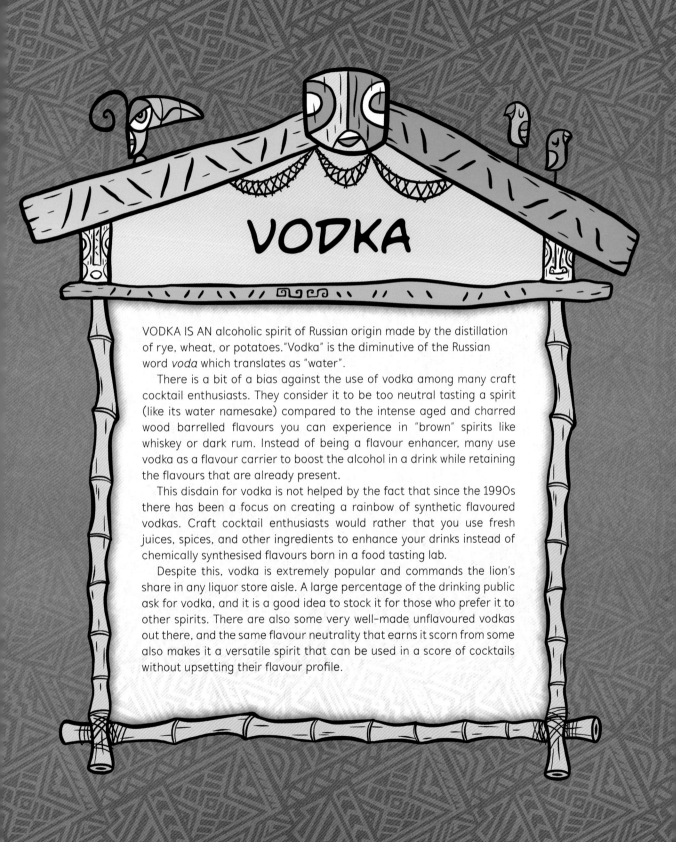

VODKA

VODKA IS AN alcoholic spirit of Russian origin made by the distillation of rye, wheat, or potatoes. "Vodka" is the diminutive of the Russian word *voda* which translates as "water".

There is a bit of a bias against the use of vodka among many craft cocktail enthusiasts. They consider it to be too neutral tasting a spirit (like its water namesake) compared to the intense aged and charred wood barrelled flavours you can experience in "brown" spirits like whiskey or dark rum. Instead of being a flavour enhancer, many use vodka as a flavour carrier to boost the alcohol in a drink while retaining the flavours that are already present.

This disdain for vodka is not helped by the fact that since the 1990s there has been a focus on creating a rainbow of synthetic flavoured vodkas. Craft cocktail enthusiasts would rather that you use fresh juices, spices, and other ingredients to enhance your drinks instead of chemically synthesised flavours born in a food tasting lab.

Despite this, vodka is extremely popular and commands the lion's share in any liquor store aisle. A large percentage of the drinking public ask for vodka, and it is a good idea to stock it for those who prefer it to other spirits. There are also some very well-made unflavoured vodkas out there, and the same flavour neutrality that earns it scorn from some also makes it a versatile spirit that can be used in a score of cocktails without upsetting their flavour profile.

Bachelor Number Two

Take yourself way back: the year 1965, the TV network, the American Broadcasting System, the show *The Dating Game*, the host Jim Lange. Who will be the lucky bachelor? One, two or three? Sip on this Kelly cocktail, and we think you'll agree you made a wise decision.

2 oz Grey Goose Vodka

¼ oz Dolin Vermouth de Chambéry Dry

1 oz Pavan Grappa Liqueur

A squeeze of Lemon

3 drops Fee Brothers Orange Bitters

TO SERVE
Shake the ingredients in a tin with cubed ice and then strain into a martini glass that's been pre-chilled. Garnish with a fresh lemon twist.

STRENGTH SCALE

Black Cat Juice

Created by Tom for a Halloween past. Many drinks that call themselves "black" are usually just dark green or purple. They try to achieve blackness by using blue curaçao or sambuca or other dyed liquors but fall short. Blavod makes a vodka that is literally black, so this drink should not be a problem if you have the ingredients.

In case you can't source Blavod vodka, you might want to experiment with activated charcoal which some use to achieve the same effect. Be warned, though — activated charcoal might interfere with some medications due to its absorbent properties. So, be cautious!

1½ oz Blavod Black Vodka

1 oz Freshly Squeezed Lime Juice

1 oz Bénédictine & Brandy (B&B)

1 oz Orgeat Almond Syrup

1 oz Fresh Cherry Juice (Not Syrup)

¼ tsp of powdered activated charcoal if using this as an addition to a regular clear vodka.

TO SERVE
Build in a lowball double rocks glass and add crushed ice, then move to tin and shake before returning to the rocks glass. Garnish with cherries on a paper umbrella.

STRENGTH SCALE

Black Cat Juice

The Fickett

Dan-O's Day Off

It's the end of the mid-century... What would Danno, from the television show *Hawaii Five-O*, drink on his day off? Vodka! Danno drank Smirnoff. Try this cocktail with your favourite vodka — you call it. The citrus flavours are in there. Very refreshing. "Book 'em, Danno!" Created by Kelly and inspired by the song from the Tikiyaki Orchestra's album, *Swingin' Sounds for the Jungle Jetset*.

2 oz Smirnoff Vodka

½ oz Cointreau Orange Liqueur

1 oz Simple Syrup

1 oz White Grapefruit Juice

1 oz Freshly Squeezed Lemon Juice

1 oz Club Soda

5 dashes of Angostura Bitters

TO SERVE
Shake with crushed ice and serve tall in a footed pilsner or in your favourite tiki mug. Garnish with a tall umbrella spear including two cherries, pineapple wedge, and a lime wedge.

STRENGTH SCALE

The Fickett

Created by Kelly. A fresh and delightful cocktail that is like receiving a floral bouquet. Inspired by the architecture of Edward H. Fickett, who designed more than 60,000 post-war homes, while pioneering many of the concepts considered synonymous with California Modernism. The popular publication *Better Homes And Gardens* declared Fickett "The Frank Lloyd Wright of the 1950s".

1½ oz Vodka (Fair Quinoa or Stolichnaya)

1 large muddled Basil Leaf

½ oz Homemade Lavender Syrup

TO SERVE
Shake all the ingredients with ice. Then strain into a stemmed glass or serve straight up with a sugar rim. Top with a citrus foam (lemon/lime, heavy cream).

STRENGTH SCALE

Honey Bee Waltz

A refreshing summer drink by Kelly that can be sipped as is or sweetened as much as you like by stirring in the honeycomb. We advise using pure clover honey to start, but if you feel daring, you can visit your local beekeeper and sample other varieties, such as wildflower honey, heather honey or lavender honey. When it comes to craft cocktails, never be satisfied with what you can find at the grocery store. Have an adventure, waltz around, and see what the buzz is all about!

¾ oz Chopin Vodka

½ oz Veevaçai Spirit

½ oz Homemade Honey Mix

½ oz Marie Brizard Pear William Liqueur

½ oz Freshly Squeezed Lemon Juice

TO SERVE
Shake with crushed ice and serve in a lowball glass with a chunk of honeycomb and a cherry on a skewer.

STRENGTH SCALE

Kāmaguna

In Buddhism, *Kāmaguna* means "strings of sensuality" which touch on the five physical senses: visible objects, sounds, aromas, flavours, and tactile sensations. It usually refers to sense experiences that, like the strings of a lute when plucked, give rise to pleasurable feelings. Created by Kelly to fine-tune your Kundalini (ones primal energy located at the base of the spine).

¾ oz Zen Green Tea Liqueur

1½ oz Han Vodka

2 Kumquats halved, squeezed, and dropped in

¼ oz Domaine De Canton Ginger Liqueur

A splash of Soda Water

TO SERVE
Squeeze the kumquats and cut them in half. Add them to a shaker tin with the rest of the ingredients.

STRENGTH SCALE

Honey Bee Waltz

Sicilian Vendetta

Sicilian Vendetta

A vendetta is a blood feud in which the family of a murdered person seeks vengeance on the murderer or the murderer's family. With its long history of bloodshed and where the mafia originated, Sicily is often thought of as the home of the vendetta. And, as most blood oranges are grown in Sicily, it's not hard to see a symbolic connection. Careful of this cocktail as each sip will lead to a compulsive need to drink more, and the juice will flow!

1 oz Solerno Blood Orange Liqueur

1 oz John D. Taylor's Velvet Falernum

2 oz Punzoné Vodka

1 oz Freshly Squeezed Lime Juice

4 shakes of Fee Brothers Aztec Chocolate Bitters

TO SERVE
Shake with crushed ice and serve in lowball glass with a wheel of blood orange pierced and held in place by a sword-shaped cocktail pick.

STRENGTH SCALE

Silk Road

Created by Kelly and inspired by the ancient network of trade routes that connected Asia with the Middle East and Europe. This drink is opalescent pink and soft as silk.

1½ oz Beluga Noble Russian Vodka

½ oz PAMA Pomegranate Liqueur

1 oz Absolut Mandarin Vodka

¼ oz Medium Light Agave Syrup

½ oz Freshly Squeezed Lemon Juice

A splash of Club Soda

TO SERVE
Shake with ice and strain into a chilled cocktail glass. Garnish with a long twist of lemon across the top.

STRENGTH SCALE

Vostok Cocktail

This is a Kelly original inspired by another famous space flight. The Vostok (Russian: Восток, translated as East) was a type of spacecraft built by the Soviet Union. The first human spaceflight in history was accomplished with this spacecraft on April 12th, 1961, by Soviet cosmonaut Yuri Gagarin.

2½ oz Stolichnaya Vodka

¼ oz Freshly Squeezed Lime Juice

¼ oz Homemade Hibiscus Syrup

½ oz Torani Passionfruit Syrup

¼ oz St. Germain Elderflower Liqueur

TO SERVE
Shake with crushed ice and serve in a collins glass.

STRENGTH SCALE

Watermelon Wanga

A *wanga* is a curse or spell performed by a Voodoo witch doctor or *Bokor*. This spell is particularly powerful and will leave you unable to do anything but lounge and sip your drink while you enjoy an island breeze. Created by Tom as a refreshing summer treat.

2 oz Fresh Watermelon Juice

½ oz Clover Honey Syrup

1 oz Freshly Squeezed Lemon Juice

¼ oz St Germain Elderflower Liqueur

1 oz Club Soda

2½ oz Grey Goose Vodka

TO SERVE
Shake with crushed ice, serve in a lowball glass, and garnish with a sprig of mint.

STRENGTH SCALE

Vostok Cocktail

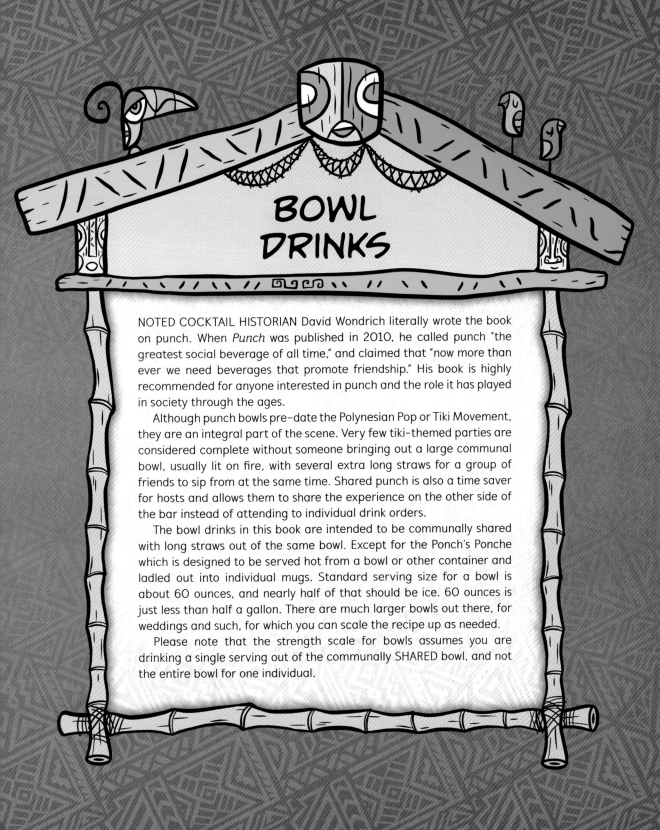

BOWL DRINKS

NOTED COCKTAIL HISTORIAN David Wondrich literally wrote the book on punch. When *Punch* was published in 2010, he called punch "the greatest social beverage of all time," and claimed that "now more than ever we need beverages that promote friendship." His book is highly recommended for anyone interested in punch and the role it has played in society through the ages.

Although punch bowls pre-date the Polynesian Pop or Tiki Movement, they are an integral part of the scene. Very few tiki-themed parties are considered complete without someone bringing out a large communal bowl, usually lit on fire, with several extra long straws for a group of friends to sip from at the same time. Shared punch is also a time saver for hosts and allows them to share the experience on the other side of the bar instead of attending to individual drink orders.

The bowl drinks in this book are intended to be communally shared with long straws out of the same bowl. Except for the Ponch's Ponche which is designed to be served hot from a bowl or other container and ladled out into individual mugs. Standard serving size for a bowl is about 60 ounces, and nearly half of that should be ice. 60 ounces is just less than half a gallon. There are much larger bowls out there, for weddings and such, for which you can scale the recipe up as needed.

Please note that the strength scale for bowls assumes you are drinking a single serving out of the communally SHARED bowl, and not the entire bowl for one individual.

Kon Tiki Rain Bowl

Kelly and Tom invented this in 2009. We didn't have a name for it when it was first made at Grog's (Ernie Keen's) during a travelling Rumpus Room. The following weekend, however, at the Tonga Hut in North Hollywood, Elvis Presley's song "Cold Kentucky Rain" was playing and Grog suggested the name Kon-Tiki Rain as a humorous riff, and the name stuck.

3 oz Cruzan Vanilla Rum

6 oz Barbancourt (three-star) Rum

4½ oz Domaine de Canton Ginger Liqueur

6 oz Orgeat Almond Syrup

¾ oz Homemade Pimento Allspice Syrup

4½ oz Freshly Squeezed Lemon Juice

3 oz Freshly Squeezed Lime Juice

3 splashes Club Soda

3 floats Lemon Hart Regular 80 Proof Demerara Rum

TO SERVE

Makes about 33 oz and should be served in a 60 oz bowl with the remainder of the bowl filled with crushed ice. Garnish with fresh mint sprigs, cherries, lemon wedges, and lime wedges. Can be lit on fire using a half lime shell with a sugar cube coated with a small amount of 151 overproof rum or lemon juice extract. For a fire show, simply sprinkle a small amount of dusted cinnamon powder and watch the sparks fly.

STRENGTH SCALE

Luau Pig Bowl

Invented by Kelly & Tom in 2009 at Kirby & Polly's Rumpus Room in La Crescenta, California. With the apple and smoke flavours, it lives up to its name.

3 dashes of Angostura Bitters

5¼ oz Homemade Black Pepper Syrup

3 oz Homemade Hibiscus Syrup

¾ oz Cinnamon Syrup

4½ oz Apple Juice

1½ oz John D. Taylor's Falernum

3 oz Pineapple Juice

3 oz Martinique or White Rum

3 oz Freshly Squeezed Lime Juice

4½ oz Lemon Hart 80 Proof Demerara Rum

3 oz Club Soda

Add almost 4 cups (28½ oz) crushed ice

TO SERVE

Makes 60 oz. Garnish with apple slices. For added bacon flavour cut up your apple slices ahead of time and jar them up with Bakon Vodka for a few weeks or go the whole hog and substitute the 3 oz of White Rum with Bakon Vodka.

STRENGTH SCALE

Luau Pig Bowl

Pele's Kiss Bowl

Pele's Kiss Bowl

Pele in Hawaiian mythology is the goddess of fire, and volcanoes as well as the creator of the Hawaiian Islands. This drink was created by Kelly. You can see the scaled-down individual recipe on page 123.

6 oz Cruzan Coconut Rum

3 oz Cruzan Vanilla Rum

6 oz Homemade Ancho Pepper Syrup

6 oz Cracked Black Pepper Syrup

¾ oz Disaronno Almond Liqueur

3 oz Lemon Hart Demerara 151 Rum

3 oz Orange Juice

3 oz Freshly Squeezed Lime Juice

TO SERVE

Makes 30¾ oz and should be served in a 60 oz bowl with remainder filled with crushed ice. Garnish with one half of a Dragon Fruit that has the leaves licking upwards to mimic flames. Place a sugar cube soaked in overproof rum or lemon extract on top of the leaves and light on fire. Shower with cinnamon powder for sparks! All hail Pele! Her fiery kiss is tempered with cool love. The sweet rums, coconut and vanilla come together but not for long, Pele is angry, and with this anger comes Lemon Hart 151 Rum. Sweetness is spun into a unique spicy cocktail.

STRENGTH SCALE

Pohō Moku Bowl

Created by Kelly. Evokes a lingering breeze from the islands. Inspired by the Tikiyaki Orchestra's song of the same name.

9 oz Cruzan Vanilla Rum

3 oz Grand Marnier Orange Liqueur

3 oz Domaine de Canton Ginger Liqueur

3 oz Homemade Ancho Chili Pepper Syrup

1½ oz Torani Passionfruit Syrup

4½ oz Freshly Squeezed Lemon Juice

4½ oz Freshly Squeezed Lime Juice

6 oz Soda Water

TO SERVE

Makes almost 35 oz. Serve in 60 oz bowl with the remainder of the bowl filled with crushed ice. Garnish with limes and cherries.

This drink is often served on fire using a half spent lime shell with sugar cube coated with a small amount of 151 overproof rum or lemon juice extract. For a fire show sprinkle a small amount of dusted cinnamon powder and watch the sparks fly.

STRENGTH SCALE

Ponch's Ponche Bowl

This is Tom's take on a traditional ponche. Traditionally this is made in large batches (5 gallons) and served hot throughout the evening. With its roots in the traditional Mexican Christmas punch, this is exactly what you would expect Eric Estrada's character, Frank "Ponch" Poncherello, to kick back with after a hard day on the job, busting bad guys with the other officers of California Highway Patrol, in the classic television show *CHiPs*.

6½ oz Tres Generaciones Anejo Tequila

13 oz Remy Martin Cognac

3¼ oz Nocello Walnut Liqueur

3¼ oz Hum Hibiscus Liqueur

¼ teaspoon of Pernod

3¼ oz Cinnamon Syrup

6½ oz Freshly Squeezed Lemon Juice

22¾ oz Fresh Apple Cider (non-alcoholic)

TO SERVE
Makes slightly less than 60 oz. Ladle out of large crock-pot or other hot container and serve while hot in a coffee mug with an apple slice as garnish.

STRENGTH SCALE

Scorpion Prohibido Bowl

A Kelly cocktail inspired by the classic Scorpion Bowl, this drink trades out gin for genever and subs a dark Jamaican rum for the more common Puerto Rican Gold Rum. Also added is some pimento syrup and lime instead of lemon. Different but familiar and very delicious. The Scorpion Prohibido (Forbidden Scorpion) has a bit of a sting but goes down smooth.

5 oz Smith and Cross Jamaican Rum

5 oz Bols Genever

2½ oz Homemade Pimento Syrup

3¾ oz Christian Brothers Brandy

2½ oz Orgeat Almond Syrup

5 oz Torani Passionfruit Syrup

5 oz Orange Juice

3¾ oz Freshly Squeezed Lime Juice

TO SERVE
Makes almost 33 oz of cocktail. Add to 60 oz bowl and fill the remainder with crushed ice. Garnish with several long strips of orange peel.

STRENGTH SCALE

Ponch's Ponche Bowl

Trader Tom's Wayward Rum Barrel Bowl

Trader Tom's Rum Punch Bowl

Tom invented this at the Rumpus Room in La Crescenta, California. This punch is inspired by traditional red-coloured Jamaican rum punches, but instead of grenadine, this punch gets its lovely red colouring from blood orange syrup. Also, instead of the more common pineapple and orange juice mix blend, Tom uses the much heavier guava nectar. El Dorado is a premium touch and much more extravagant than the "well" rums used to make your typical Jamaican punch, but occasionally, you need to indulge yourself! One thing is for sure, there was never any punch left in the punch bowl at the end of the evening...

6 oz El Dorado 12-Year-Old Demerara Rum

3 oz Coruba Dark Jamaican Rum

1½ oz Monin Blood Orange Syrup

9 oz Freshly Squeezed Lime Juice

3 oz Kern's Farm Guava Nectar

3 oz BG Reynolds Orgeat Almond Syrup

3 oz Soda Water

1½ oz BG Reynolds Cinnamon Syrup

Add almost 4 cups (30 oz) Crushed Ice

TO SERVE
Garnish with several mint sprigs.
Makes 60 oz.

STRENGTH SCALE

Trader Tom's Wayward Rum Barrel Bowl

Trader Tom has so many cocktail vessels that sometimes they get lost, drifting around in the turbulent waters of his tiki bar until they are re-discovered and put to good use. Here is a recipe he came up with to re-baptise a prodigal rum barrel that went missing and then returned to the fold.

4 oz Panama-Pacific 9 Year Rum

4 oz Appleton 12 Year Dark Jamaican

4 oz Ed Hamilton 151 Overproof Demerara

2 oz St. Elizabeth's Pimento Liqueur

3 oz BG Reynolds Passionfruit Syrup

3 oz Clover Honey Syrup Mix

4 oz Fresh Orange Juice

8 oz Fresh Lime Juice

24 shakes (¼ tsp) Angostura Bitters

24 drops (¼ tsp) Letherbee Charred Oak Absinthe

TO SERVE
Makes about 32 oz. Add to a 60 oz metal bowl and fill the remainder with crushed ice, swizzle with a top-down mixer (sometimes called a "spindle blender" and is like what you would use to make an old-fashioned milkshake.) and then empty into your final container, such as large ceramic rum barrel.

STRENGTH SCALE

Voluptuous Virgin Bowl

This is Trader Tom's twist on the traditional Vicious Virgin invented by Don the Beachcomber back in the 1940s. Made with rum from the Virgin Islands. Too many and it ain't half vicious!

7 oz Freshly Squeezed Lime Juice

5 oz Pierre Ferrand Dry Curaçao

2½ oz BG Reynolds Falernum Syrup

1½ oz Monin Cherry Syrup

4 oz El Dorado 12-Year-Old Demerara Rum

8 oz Cruzan Single Barrel Rum
(from the US Virgin Islands)

4 cups crushed ice (8 oz per cup = 32 oz)

TO SERVE
Add a splash of soda water and garnish with half a dozen premium cherries from a jar (such as Tillen Farms Bada Bing dark cherries). Makes enough for a full 60 oz bowl.

STRENGTH SCALE

Volcano Cooler Bowl

This was invented by Tom at the Rumpus Room in La Crescenta, California. If you have a carton of POG (Pineapple/Orange juice/Guava), you may use that without having to measure out three different juices. This is a very refreshing red punch drink and proved very popular with the rumpusing crowd.

3 oz Cruzan White Rum

3 oz Coruba Dark Jamaican Rum

3 oz Kern's Farm Guava Nectar

6 oz Freshly Squeezed Lemon Juice

3 oz No-Pulp Orange Juice

3 oz Unsweetened Pineapple Juice

3 oz Soda Water

3 oz Monin Blood Orange Syrup

3 oz BG Reynolds Orgeat Almond Syrup

Add almost 4 cups (30 oz) crushed ice

TO SERVE
Garnish with pineapple rings speared through with cherries in the middle. Makes 60 oz.

STRENGTH SCALE

Voluptuous Virgin Bowl

Syrups and Infusions

Commercial tiki bars boast a wide array of rums, often with hundreds of bottles from all over the world. The humble home bar is governed by a much tighter budget. Home bar owners usually stock the makings for a few of their favourite drinks but often grow frustrated, wanting to stretch their liquor pantry to get more variety and "bang for their buck."

An inexpensive way to diversify your cocktail offerings without spending so much on alcohol is to have a wider array of mixers on hand. I'm not talking about what you can find at your typical neighbourhood store, although that's a start. Commercial mixers have gotten better over the years, but if you challenge yourself to source fresh ingredients, the sky is the limit.

There are hundreds of different kinds of fruits and fruit juices out there, but mainstream grocery stores stock a fraction of that. Go further afield and check farmer's markets or niche ethnic shops. You'll be happy you did. Feel free to experiment with fresh herbs and spices and let your imagination be your guide. With these fresh ingredients, you can then prepare juices, garnishes, syrups, bitters, and infusions that will WOW your guests.

Syrup, in particular, is an economical alternative because sugar and water are much less expensive than buying more booze. A properly prepared syrup can last for weeks and give an exotic flavouring that will breathe new life into your home drink menu. You will have no doubt noticed that the recipes in this book make heavy use of flavoured syrups.

When Tom and Kelly first started collaborating, about the only commercially available cane sugar syrups were Torani and Monin (we're not including the corn syrup based mixers as they usually have too many chemicals and people prefer more natural products). These two companies boasted a long list of flavours online but, in actuality, retailers were mostly stocking only coffee-related flavours, such as hazelnut

and vanilla. Only speciality shops offered a wider assortment and usually for premium prices. Online blogs and boards, especially *Tiki Central*, revealed just how inexpensive it was to create your own. The emphasis with tiki cocktails remains with those syrups needed to create classic tiki cocktails, such as orgeat and grenadine. The online recipes and those in Beachbum Berry's books for these classic syrups are solid and worth your attention. We won't try to re-invent the wheel or repeat the recipes for all the classics. Below, however, you will find some of our favourite syrups (and other infusions). We are known for incorporating uncommon flavours into our cocktails.

- Kelly is a fan of the "pot and bungee cord with flour sack" method of making syrup. For more detail, please see the Cracked Black Pepper recipe on p239. Tom usually uses a pot with cheesecloth and rubber bands, but as you do more and more syrups, you will find your own shortcuts and preferred methods, greatly depending on what you have available around the house.

- You can put your syrups and infusions in many different containers, from recycled liquor bottles to mason jars. Kelly tends to use recycled 1-litre rum bottles which is very "green". If you make lots of rum drinks you never really run out of these. These 1-litre bottles are about 4.2 cups (33.6 oz). Tom prefers the Bormioli Rocco Giara clear glass bottles with ceramic and rubber stoppers that have a wire swing-away "cage" similar to Grolsch beer bottles. These bottles hold 33¾ oz. Many of Tom's syrup recipes are scaled to make 9 cups (72 oz) which would be two full Bormioli bottles and a little over a half cup (4½ oz) to use immediately. You can order the Bormioli bottles online or buy them at most major retail stores.

- Whatever container(s) you use, make sure you have cleaned and sterilised it (them). Tom comes from a home brewing background and believes dishwashing detergent is too mild to completely sterilise. You don't want your syrup to go bad too soon because of contaminants after all the work you've done! He recommends going to a brewing supply store and getting some type of percarbonate. Percarbonates are a combination of sodium carbonate and hydrogen peroxide. They effectively remove dirt and deposits from all kinds of equipment. Percarbonates work with active oxygen and a mild alkali to help lift the grime. One of the best properties of the percarbonate family is that they are environmentally and septic system friendly. P.B.W. (Powdered Brewery Wash) is a percarbonate that was developed by Coors and is the highest strength of the percarbonates listed. It is very effective in dissolving stubborn stains in hard to reach places. It works well with a 30-minute soak. A 1 lb container should be enough for several washings.

- As a general rule, homemade syrups with a splash of overproof rum as a preservative agent will last for at least a month and possibly as long as three months in the refrigerator. We suggest labelling and dating them. Also, after the one-month mark make sure to check them for any sign of going bad which will appear as a cloudiness in the syrup. If there is a sign of this, dump them immediately.

ANCHO CHILLE SYRUP
10-12 dried ancho chilli peppers
6.66 cups sugar
6.66 cups water
1 oz Wray & Nephew's Overproof Rum

DIRECTIONS: Combine sugar, water, and peppers and simmer on low medium for 30-40 minutes in an uncovered pot. A few flakes of dried red peppercorn can be added for more heat as desired. When peppers are soft in 10 minutes, cut them into quarters with kitchen shears without removing from the pot. At the end of cooking time, let it cool to room temperature, then sift with a cheesecloth and pour into sterilised bottles. Top each bottle with the overproof rum and gently mix by giving the bottles a few turns. Then refrigerate until ready to use.

CHAMOMILE SYRUP
One 4 oz packet of dried chamomile
4½ cups sugar
4½ cups water
1 oz Wray & Nephew's Overproof Rum

DIRECTIONS: Dissolve water and sugar over medium heat. Once dissolved, turn up the heat, add chamomile, and bring to near boil. Let steep for three minutes, then turn down and let simmer for 30 minutes. Let cool, then strain with a cheesecloth into sterilised bottles. Top bottles with the overproof rum and gently mix by giving bottles a few turns. Then refrigerate until ready to use.

CHINESE FIVE SPICE SYRUP
4½ tablespoons of Five Spice Blend Powder
½ oz lemon juice
4½ cups sugar
4½ cups water
1 oz Wray & Nephew's Overproof Rum

DIRECTIONS: Five Spice Powder is a blend of cinnamon, cloves, fennel, star anise, and Sichuan peppercorns. Some recipes also contain ginger and nutmeg. You can buy it pre-packaged or make your own blend. Dissolve some sugar in water over a medium heat. Once dissolved, turn up the heat, add the five spice blend, and bring to near boil. Let it steep for three minutes, then turn it down and let it simmer for a full 30 minutes. After which let it cool, then strain with a cheesecloth into sterilised bottles. Top bottles with the overproof rum and gently mix by giving bottles a few turns. Then refrigerate until ready to use.

CRACKED BLACK PEPPER SYRUP
(TOM'S SIMPLE VERSION)
1 cup black peppercorns
4 pinches of red pepper flakes
4½ cups sugar
4½ cups water
1 oz Wray & Nephew's Overproof Rum

DIRECTIONS: Grind peppercorns and flakes in a coffee grinder set aside for only grinding spices (you don't want this in your coffee!). In a small saucepan over a medium heat dissolve the sugar in the water, then add pepper and bring to near boil. Let the mixture steep 3 minutes, then turn it down and let it simmer on a lower temperature for 15 to 20 minutes. Once cool sift with a cheesecloth and pour into sterilised bottles. Top bottles with the overproof rum and gently mix by giving bottles a few turns. Then refrigerate until ready to use.

CRACKED BLACK PEPPER SYRUP
(KELLY'S DETAILED VERSION)
You will be making a small batch of 1 to 2 bottles.

First go to the supermarket, in the kitchen section buy an inexpensive package of what is usually called flour sack towels. These are the dish drying towels I grew up on. The beauty of them is, flour sack towels do not shed or leave lint or residue. They are perfect for drying dishes, cleaning mirrors and windows and making simple syrup. These work better and are much cheaper than cheesecloth.

Second, get a standard size bungee cord and a 4 qt. or so big pot. Lay the Flour sackcloth over the empty pot and bungee around the pot making the flour sackcloth tight as a drumhead.

Third, follow these steps:

Step 1: Using a big pot on the stove top pour 3¼ cups of HOT water into the pot and turn fire on high. About ¼ cup or more of water will disappear into steam. This is a thicker caramelised simple syrup, for a thinner version add more water.

Step 2: Measure out 3 cups of pure cane sugar and pour it into the pot of hot water and stir until the sugar is dissolved. Do NOT buy sugar that doesn't say PURE CANE on the packaging, it might say pure sugar but from what? Beets or corn? Pure cane sugar is what you want.

Step 3: Lower your heat to medium-low. Don't scorch your sugar for it won't taste nice.

Step 4: Add 6 tablespoons or more to taste of coarse ground black pepper. If you want a stronger or lighter pepper taste adjust this measurement. I'd suggest making it spicy!!! You don't want your cocktail too sweet or boring.

Step 5: Turn your fire up a bit until you have a small rapid boil going that is turning your syrup on its own without stirring it yourself. Cover the pot and reduce the fire but keep a small boil going. Be careful not to scorch the sugar. Let it low boil for 30 minutes.

Step 6: Get another pot leaving the pot with the drumhead you made to the side for later. Get a wire type food strainer and place the pot in the sink. Carefully pour the HOT syrup through the strainer into the pot discarding the ground pepper into the trash.

Step 7: Set your pot with the drumhead into the clean sink and carefully pour the syrup you just strained onto and into the drumhead pot. The syrup will slowly seep into the pot leaving almost all the residue on top of the drumhead. Now unfasten the bungee cord and sticky cloth and lay them aside.

Step 8: Pour the syrup into a 750ml–1litre bottle or a tall Tupperware, Rubbermaid type container. Add ½ ounce less or more depending on how much syrup you have of 151 Rum for a preservative. This will last a month in the refrigerator.

IMPORTANT NOTE: If you're using a glass bottle to store your syrup fill it first with hot water and get the bottle hot, then pour out the hot water and pour the hot syrup into it, so it doesn't break! Place the bottle on hot pads or towels, not the cold counter top.

You're done! Making a bigger batch? Double it up.

In the case of all these syrups, (but especially the spicy ones like black pepper syrup) you will accidentally make them weaker or more potent than you had intended from time to time. Whatever the reason, no effort is wasted. An easy fix is to dilute your flavoured syrup by adding more unflavored simple syrup. Or increase its potency by making a stronger batch and mixing it with the weaker. Blend until you have it exactly to your taste.

FIREBALL CHERRIES

There are tons of liquor-soaked cherries available commercially, including the ever-popular Luxardo Maraschino Cherries. Tom's personal favourite happens to be cinnamon cherries made by taking Tillen Farms Pink Blush or Bada Bing Cherries and removing the syrup/juice from the jar, then replacing that liquid with a solution that is equal parts Lemon Hart 151 Overproof Rum and BG Reynold's Cinnamon Syrup. Save that cherry juice in another container to use in something else. Waste not want not. Let the cherries absorb the rum and cinnamon flavours for a few weeks, turning the jar every so often. Try one to see if they have been thoroughly infused. As an alternative one could use a cinnamon flavoured whiskey. This would only be fine if you intended to use the cherries for a whiskey-based drink. For a rum cocktail the above solution tends to work best.

GINGER SYRUP

1 big handful of freshly peeled and cubed ginger root
4½ cups sugar
4½ cups water
1 oz Wray & Nephew's Overproof Rum

DIRECTIONS: Dissolve sugar into water over medium heat. Once dissolved, turn up the heat, add ginger, and bring to a near boil. Let steep for three minutes, then turn down and let simmer for 30 minutes. Let cool, then strain with cheesecloth into sterilised bottles. Top bottles with the overproof rum and gently mix by giving the bottles a few turns. Then refrigerate until ready to use.

HIBISCUS SYRUP

4 packages of Jamaica Brand dried hibiscus flowers
10 cups of sugar
10 cups of water
1 juiced lemon
3 oz Wray & Nephew's Overproof Rum

DIRECTIONS: Dissolve sugar into water over a medium heat, add the flowers and lemon juice, then bring to a boil. Let steep four minutes. Let cool, then sieve the flowers and pour the syrup into bottles that have been sterilised. Top each bottle with 1 oz of overproof rum and gently mix by giving each bottle a few turns. Then refrigerate until ready to use.

LAVENDER SYRUP

4 oz packet of dried lavender
4½ cups sugar
4½ cups water
1 oz Wray & Nephew's Overproof Rum

DIRECTIONS: Dissolve sugar into water over medium heat. Once dissolved, turn up the heat, add the dried lavender, and bring to a near boil. Let steep for three minutes, then turn down and let simmer for 30 minutes. Let cool, then strain with a cheesecloth into sterilised bottles. Top bottles with the overproof rum and gently mix by giving bottles a few turns. Then refrigerate until ready to use.

LEMONGRASS SYRUP

4 oz packet of dried lemongrass
4½ cups sugar
4½ cups water
1 oz Wray & Nephew's Overproof Rum

DIRECTIONS: Dissolve sugar into water over a medium heat. Once dissolved, turn up the heat, add the lemongrass, and bring to a near boil. Let the mixture steep for three minutes, then turn it down and let it simmer for 30 minutes. Let cool, then strain it with a cheesecloth into sterilised bottles. Top the bottles with the overproof rum and gently mix by giving the bottles a few turns. Then refrigerate until ready to use.

PEANUT ORGEAT SYRUP

2 cups roasted and unsalted peanuts
1½ cups sugar
1¼ cups water
1 tsp. orange flower water
1 oz Wray & Nephew Overproof Rum

DIRECTIONS: Pulverise the peanuts in a food processor. Meanwhile, combine the sugar and water in a saucepan over a medium heat, constantly stirring until the sugar dissolves. Allow the mixture to boil for three minutes, then add the peanuts. Lower the heat, allowing the mixture to simmer for several more minutes, then gradually increase the temperature. When the mixture is about to boil, remove from the heat, and cover. Let the mixture cool, then strain it through a cheesecloth. Add the orange flower water and the overproof rum. Keep for up to two weeks in the refrigerator.

PIMENTO (ALLSPICE) SYRUP
5 tablespoons ground pimento (allspice) berries
3 cups sugar
4½ cups water
2 oz Lemon Hart 151 Rum

DIRECTIONS: Dissolve sugar into water over medium heat. Once dissolved, turn up the heat, add the pimento, and bring to a near boil. Let steep for three minutes, then turn down and let simmer for 30 minutes. Let cool, then strain with a cheesecloth into sterilised bottles. Top bottles with the overproof rum and gently mix by giving the bottles a few turns. Then refrigerate until ready to use.

NOTE: Kelly uses a 1 to 1 ratio of sugar to water for a thinner syrup, and right before she removes it from the stove, she adds 4-5 TBS of blackstrap molasses to give it a buttery flavour and more luxurious texture. She also specifies Lemon Hart 151, not just any overproof rum.

PISTACHIO SYRUP
4½ cups of shelled pistachios
4½ cups sugar
4½ cups water
1 oz Wray & Nephew's Overproof Rum

DIRECTIONS: Grind up the pistachios in a food processor. Dissolve sugar into water over a medium heat. Once dissolved, turn up the heat, add the ground pistachios, and bring to a near boil. Let steep for three minutes, then turn down and let it simmer for 45 minutes to 1 hour. Once cool strain with a metal mesh strainer and then a cheesecloth into sterilised bottles. For greener syrup, strain more finely or use a centrifuge to separate out the solids. The less you strain it, the browner it will be, but it will basically taste the same. Kelly sometimes adds a little bit of green food colouring if she feels it needs the colour to come through. Top bottles with the overproof rum and gently mix it all together by giving the bottles a few turns. Then refrigerate until ready to use.

PRICKLY PEAR CACTUS SYRUP
3 pounds prickly pears
4½ cups sugar
4½ cups water
Juice of 2 lemons
1 oz Wray & Nephew Overproof Rum

DIRECTIONS: First, remove the skins of the prickly pears by trimming the ends, making a lengthwise incision, and peeling back the outer portion with its spiky surface. Put the prickly pears in a pot and add the water to cover. Bring to a boil. Turn down the heat and let steep for 30 minutes. Then, mash the fruit with a potato masher, and separate out the seeds. Strain with a metal mesh strainer, then again with cheesecloth. Take the strained juice and pour it into a pot. Add the sugar and bring to a simmer over medium heat for 5 minutes. Let cool and add the lemon juice. Top bottles with the overproof rum and gently mix by giving the bottles a few turns. Then refrigerate until ready to use.

RHUBARB SYRUP
6 stalks of ripe red rhubarb
4½ cups sugar
4½ cups water
1 oz Wray & Nephew's Overproof Rum

DIRECTIONS: Dissolve the sugar into the water over medium heat. Once dissolved, turn up the heat, add the rhubarb (cubed up to cook faster and make straining easier), and bring to a near boil. Let steep for three minutes, then turn down and let simmer for 30 minutes. Let cool, then strain with a metal mesh sifter into sterilised bottles. The rhubarb dissolves into a very slimy mess and may take a long time to strain, but be patient. Top bottles with the overproof rum and gently mix by giving the bottles a few turns. Then refrigerate until ready to use.

SESAME SYRUP
Here are two different methods for making this syrup. The first way is to utilise pan or oven roasted sesame seeds. The second is to use bottled sesame seed oil. Ideal if you are in a hurry. It is more difficult, however, to force the bottled oil into a suspension. Despite this, if time is short it is still a quick and easy alternative. If you notice the oil separating, shake more vigorously.

SESAME SYRUP
ROASTED SEEDS (VARIANT A): Spread two cups
of sesame seeds out on a baking sheet and roast at 350°F (175°C) until lightly toasted, about 8-10 minutes. Alternatively, you can roast them in a pan on the stovetop on medium high until they have some colour and the essential oils are "sweating" out.

2 cups sesame seeds
2 cups sugar
2 cups water
1 oz Wray & Nephew's Overproof Rum

DIRECTIONS: Dissolve sugar into water over a medium heat. Once dissolved, turn up the heat, add the roasted seeds, and bring to anear boil. Let steep for three minutes, then turn down and let simmer for 15 minutes. Let cool, then strain with a cheesecloth into sterilised bottles. Top bottles with the overproof rum and gently mix by giving the bottles a few turns. Then refrigerate until ready to use.

BOTTLED SESAME OIL (VARIANT B)
2 oz bottled sesame oil
2 cups sugar
2 cups water
1 oz Wray & Nephew's Overproof Rum

DIRECTIONS: Dissolve the sugar into the water over a medium heat. Once dissolved, turn up the heat, add the sesame oil, and bring to a boil. Let steep for three minutes, then turn down and let simmer for 15 minutes. Let cool, then top bottles with the overproof rum and gently mix by giving the bottles a few turns. Then refrigerate until ready to use. There will be separation, and you will need to shake the bottled syrup before use and shake your cocktails vigorously so as not to have a film of oil rise to the top of your drinks.

SIMPLE SYRUP
Simple syrup consists of equal parts sugar and water that have been blended by dissolving the sugar in a saucepan into the water on a medium heat, then bringing the solution to a near boil and letting it cool before adding an ounce of overproof rum or other overproof distillate as a preservative. One can use a high powered mixer to blend this syrup together, eschewing the heat altogether.

We urge you to use pure cane sugar, not sugar derived from beats. If you have impurities, then you might find that crystallisation happens in the container, but if you are careful, this should not be a concern. Making a new batch is also straightforward. Simple even.

There are other varieties of simple syrup, including Rock Candy Syrup which is made of 2 parts sugar to 1-part water. It is harder to make and to keep from going bad but is essential for some cocktails. There are several commercial varieties. Also of note is Gomme Syrup which is made using gum arabic. Gomme Syrup gives a thicker mouthfeel to drinks and a saucier texture. You can order gum arabic as a powder if you are curious to experiment with it. There are a couple of companies that have produced Gomme Syrup, but it is the hardest to commercially source.

TAMARIND SYRUP
2 cups of tamarind pods
4½ cups sugar
4½ cups water
1 oz Wray & Nephew's Overproof Rum

DIRECTIONS: Pre-soak the tamarind pods. Then remove the hard outer shell and hard seeds and dispose of them.

Dissolve sugar into water over a medium heat. Once dissolved, turn up the heat, add the cleaned interior of the tamarind pods, and bring to a near boil. Steep for three minutes, then turn it down and let simmer for 30 minutes. Let it cool, then strain with a metal mesh sifter and then a cheesecloth into sterilised bottles. Top bottles with the overproof rum and gently mix by giving the bottles a few turns. Then refrigerate until ready to use.

DATE FRUIT PUREE
Year-round you can usually find fresh dates. Buy more than you need because after you puree them, they will keep in your freezer for about six months. Place about 10 pitted dates in a food processor or high powered blender, add ¼ cup warm water. Blend to a slightly chunky texture, adding small amounts of extra water as required. Avoid making it to smooth. You want some of the particles to filter into the cocktail when you strain it into the glass. Place what you won't be using in a plastic freezer bag and place it in the freezer.

ZACAPA FOAM

Using shaker tin or whip cream nitrous charger add half a fresh egg white or purchase pasteurised egg whites. In a small carton, add 1½ oz of Zacapa Rum, ½ oz of cream, 2 Tbs of cane sugar and shake.

SPECIAL SUMMER PORT REDUCTION

1 part weak Simple Syrup (60% water/40% sugar) to 1 part Ruby Port reduced at medium heat for 15 minutes. Kelly uses Quinta do Infantado Ruby Port.

PLANTATION

OVERPROOF 69%

69% OVERPROOF
ARTISANAL RUM

O.F.T.D.
OLD FASHIONED TRADITIONAL DARK

MASTER BLENDER
at the Château de Bonbonnet

BLEND OF RUMS FROM

69% ALC.BY VOL. Product of BA

PLANTATION

20th
ANNIVERSARY

XO

DAGGER
PUNCH BRAND

LIGHTWEIGHT PACK
WITH
BUILT-IN POURER

IMPORTED

DAGGER
PUNCH ★ BRAND
DARK
JAMAICA RUM

43.8%
ALC/VOL   1.75L

PRODUCT OF JAMAICA

JAMAICA 1891   LONDON 1862   PARIS 1878

J. WRAY & NEPHEW LTD
DISTILLERS & BLENDERS SINCE 1825
KINGSTON, JAMAICA WEST INDIES

SINGLE BAR
ESTATE
RUM

RUZAN
GLE BARREL
ESTATE
RUM

LED, AGED & CRAFTED BY
ZAN RUM DISTILLERY CO.
DIAMOND, ST. CROIX, V.I.

From Well To Top Shelf

AN ADJUSTMENT GUIDE FOR THE FRUGAL MIXOLOGIST IN AMERICAN DOLLARS AND BRITISH POUNDS

- This is just an example of rums, not other spirits, and the nearly 100 or so listed here are only the tip of the iceberg. Not all of these will be available in your area. Due to the constant requests from rum drinkers to distributors, salesmen and local liquor boards, however, each year is seeing more of these brands available to a wider audience. Online sources have also closed the gap in recent years. Keep fighting the good fight!

- This way of ranking rums simplifies some pretty big factors. There are many wonderful sources out there to help you explore rums further. This is not a perfect list, but a beginner guide meant as a jumping-off point into the wild world of rum.

- We're sure that many people will dispute any such list, but we thought it would be useful to see an example of how people might adjust their rums on a sliding scale from top shelf to bottom shelf depending on their budget. Naturally, prices and products change from year to year, so you must do a little research to stay current. This is just a limited snapshot. A thorough list of rums would be much longer, and there are plenty of websites you can go to for rum reviews, including the Ministry of Rum, Rum Dood, Republic of Rum Blogspot, 5 Minutes of Rum, Rum Ratings, and numerous threads on Tiki Central.

- Additionally, purists might claim that replacing a top-shelf ingredient with a bottom shelf ingredient changes its character so much that it is no longer the same drink! In some cases, this is true. But, in some cases the difference is negligible, and in a few rare cases the lower shelf ingredients play better together, and you can save quite a bit of money by going with a less expensive spirit. After having to think on our feet at so many differently equipped home bars over the years, we've had to make millions of these adjustments on the fly. Sometimes it makes a big difference and sometimes not. Happy experimenting!

- The standard American sized bottle is 750 ml which would translate to 75 cl. In the EU the standard size of a spirit bottles is 70 cl. So, at least for now, there is a difference between the bottling sizes, and this should be noted when considering the price point value for various brands. You also might want to look for the small "mini bottles" if trying a new rum for the first time. This way you avoid purchasing a large bottle that may only gather dust.

OVERPROOF RUM

TOP SHELF Lost Spirits Cuban 151 ($48-$65 for 750ml / Not available in the UK)

Lemon Hart 151 ($27-$35 for 750ml / Not available in the UK)

Hamilton 151 ($28-$30 for 750ml / Not available in the UK)

Plantation O.F.T.D. 138 Proof ($28 for 1L or £39 for 70cl)

MIDDLE SHELF Don Q 151 ($24 for 750ml or £36 for 70cl)

BOTTOM SHELF El Dorado 151 ($18-$23 for 750ml / Not available in the UK)

Cruzan 151 ($18-$21 for 750ml / Not available in the UK)

Wray & Nephew ($18-$22 for 750ml or £28 for 70cl)

Admiral Vernon's Old J Tiki Fire Spiced (Not available in the US £36 for 70cl)

DEMERARA RUM (FROM GUYANA)

TOP SHELF El Dorado Reserve 21 ($120 for 750ml or £84 for 70cl)

MIDDLE SHELF El Dorado 12 ($25-35 for 750ml or £36 for 70cl)

Hamilton 86 ($23-25 for 750ml / Not available in the UK)

Lemon Hart 80 Proof ($24 for $750 ml / Not available in the UK)

BOTTOM SHELF El Dorado 8 ($16-25 for 750ml or £28 for 70cl)

Skipper Demerara Dark Rum ($27 for 750ml or £20 for 70cl)

OVD or Old Vatted Demerara (Not currently available in the US or £20 for 70cl)

BLACKSTRAP MOLASSES RUM*

TOP SHELF Royal Jamaican Blackstrap Dark ($20 for 750ml / Not available in the UK)

MIDDLE SHELF Cruzan Blackstrap ($13-$19 for 750ml / Not available in the UK)

* Kraken Black Spiced Rum or Gosling's Black Seal can sub if above
are not available.

NAVY RUM

EXTREME TOP SHELF Black Tot (Not currently available in the US or £641 for 70cl)

TOP SHELF Lost Spirits Navy Rum 136 Proof ($55-$65 for 750ml / Not available in the UK)

Pusser's 15-Year-Old Rum ($50 for 750 ml or £50 for 70cl)

Pusser's Gunpowder/109 Proof ($40 for 750 ml or £37 for 70cl)

MIDDLE SHELF Pusser's British Navy Rum ($24-$30 for 750ml or £24 for 70cl)

Woods 100 Old Navy (Not currently available in the US or £28 for 70cl)

BOTTOM SHELF Whaler's Dark Rum ($11-$19 for 750ml / Not available in the UK)

Lamb's Navy (Not currently available in the US or £16 for 70cl)

DARK RUM

EXTREME TOP SHELF Appleton Estate Joy 25 Year Old Jamaican Rum ($210 for 750 ml or £220 for 1L)

TOP SHELF Goslings Old Rum ($51- $73 for 750ml or £55 for 70cl)

Vizcaya VXOP Cask No. 21 Rum ($36-$41 for 750ml / Not available in the UK)

Mount Gay XO Rum ($38- $50 for 750ml or £41 for 70cl)

Smith & Cross ($24-$35 for 750ml / Not available in the UK)

Appleton Estate Extra 12 Year Rum ($29-$36 for 750ml or £35 for 70cl)

Doctor Bird Jamaican Rum ($24.50-$25 for 750ml / Not available in the UK)

Kōloa Kaua'i Dark Rum ($35-$40 for 750ml / Not available in the UK)

MIDDLE SHELF Angostura 7-Year Old Dark ($21-$27 for 750ml or £29 for 70cl)

Meyers's Dark ($19-$24 for 750ml / Not available in the UK)

Coruba Dark ($15-19 for 750ml / Not available in the UK)

BOTTOM SHELF Gosling's Black Seal ($17–$20 for 750ml or £20–25 for 70cl)
Trader Vic's Dark ($17–$19 for 750ml / Not available in the UK)
Bacardi Black ($15–$16 for 750ml or £23 for 70cl)

GOLD RUM (FROM A VARIETY OF PLACES)

TOP SHELF Foursquare Criterion Limited Edition (Not available in the US or £57 for 70cl)
Panama Pacific 9-Year-Old Rum ($28–$30 for 750ml / Not available in the UK)
Foursquare 9-Year Port Cask Finish ($35 for 750ml / Not available in the UK)
Doorly's 12-Year ($23–25 for 750 ml or £59 for 1L)
Ron Del Barrilito 3 Star ($38 for 750ml / Not available in the UK)
R.L. Seale's 10 Year ($20–22 for 750ml or £41 for 70cl or £59 for 1L)
Brugal 1888 ($46 for 750 ml or £41 for 1L)
Cruzan Single Barrel ($25–$30 for 750ml / Not available in the UK)
English Harbour 5 Year ($28 for 750ml / Not available in the UK)
Chairman's Reserve St. Lucia Gold Rum ($25 for 750ml or £26 for 70cl)
MIDDLE SHELF Bacardi 8 ($23–$30 for 750ml or £30 for 70cl)
Mount Gay Eclipse Rum ($19– $23 for 750ml or £24 for 70cl)
Appleton Estate VX ($18–$21 for 750ml or £33 for 1L)
Kōloa Kaua'i Gold Rum ($35–$40 for 750ml / Not available in the UK)
BOTTOM SHELF Cruzan Estate Dark/ Aged Rum ($12–$13 for 750ml / Not available in the UK)

MARTINIQUE AMBER RUM

TOP SHELF Clement XO ($55 for 750ml or £60 for 1L)
MIDDLE SHELF La Favorite Rhum Amber ($46 for 1L or £24 for 70cl)
Saint James Rum Extra Old (Not currently available)
Depaz Amber Rum ($33–$40 for 750ml / Not available in the UK)
Clement V.S.O.P. ($34–$40 for 750ml or £59 for 1L)

MARTINIQUE RHUM AGRICOLE BLANC

TOP SHELF Capovilla Rhum Agricole Blanc ($60–$90 for 750ml / Not available in the UK)
Rhum JM Agricole Blanc ($35–$36 for 750ml or £30 for 70cl or £43 for 1L)
MIDDLE SHELF Rhum Clement White ($30–$32 for 750ml or £28 for 70cl or £40 for 1L)

WHITE RUM

TOP SHELF Facundo Neo Bacardi ($45–$58 for 750ml or £40 for 70cl or £58 for 1L)
Diplomatico Rum Blanco ($25–$46 for 750ml or £35 for 70cl or £51 for 1L)
Plantation Three Star ($17–$23 for 750ml or £23 for 70cl or £34 for 1L)
MIDDLE SHELF Mount Gay Rum Silver ($20–$25 for 750ml / Not available in the UK)
Selvarey White Rum ($20–$24 for 750ml / Not available in the UK)
Denizen White Rum ($18 for 750 ml / Not available in the UK)
Don Q Cristal White Rum ($13–$14 for 750ml or £24 for 70cl)
Doorly's 3 Year White Rum ($20.00 for 750 ml or £25 for 70cl or £36 for 1L)
Appleton Estate White Rum ($16–$17 for 750ml or £18 for 70cl or £25 for 1L)
BOTTOM SHELF Cruzan White ($10–$16 for 750ml / Not available in the UK)
Havana Club 3 Anos White (Not currently available in the US or £17 for 70cl)
EXTREME BOTTOM SHELF Bacardi Silver ($20–$22 for 750ml / Not available in the UK)

SPICED RUM
TOP SHELF Pusser's Spiced Rum (Not currently available in the US or £21 for 70cl)
Kōloa Kaua'i Spice ($35–$40 for 750ml / Not available in the UK)
MIDDLE SHELF Kraken Black Spiced Rum ($15–$25 for 750ml or £29 for 70cl)
BOTTOM SHELF Sailor Jerry's Spiced Rum ($20–$26 for 750ml or £20 for 70cl or £29 for 1L)
Admiral Vernon's Old J Spiced (Not currently available in the US or £18 for 70cl)
Captain Morgan's Spiced ($16–$24 for 750ml or £16 for 70cl or £24 for 1L)

COCONUT RUM
TOP SHELF Kōloa Kaua'i Coconut ($33–$35 for 750ml / Not available in the UK)
MIDDLE SHELF Cruzan Coconut ($12–$15 for 750ml / Not available in the UK)
BOTTOM SHELF Captain Morgan Parrot Bay Rum ($19–$21 for 750ml or £25 for 70cl)
Malibu Coconut Rum ($13–$20 for 750ml or £14 for 70cl or £20 for 1L)

VANILLA RUM
TOP SHELF Brinley Gold Vanilla Rum ($19–$20 for 750ml / Not available in the UK)
MIDDLE SHELF Blue Chair Bay Vanilla Rum ($18–$20 for 750ml / Not available in the UK)
Cruzan Vanilla Rum ($12–$15 for 750ml / Not available in the UK)
Rum Jumbie Vanilla (£17 for 70cl or £23 for 1L Not available in the US)

ORANGE FLAVOURED RUM
TOP SHELF Clement Creole Shrubb ($27–$36 for 750ml / Not available in the UK)
MIDDLE SHELF Cruzan Orange Rum ($14–$18 for 750ml / Not available in the UK)
BOTTOM SHELF Bacardi Orange ($13–$16 for 750ml / Not available in the UK)

There are spiced rums with a strong orange flavour available in the UK that
are mildly spiced and might sub for an orange flavoured rum but to avoid spice
altogether, one might be better off using an orange liqueur instead.

PINEAPPLE FLAVOURED RUM
TOP SHELF Plantation Stiggins's Pineapple Rum ($30–$31 for 750ml or £36 for 70cl or
£51 for 1L But Limited Distribution in the UK — only to select bars and venues.
It's delicious, and you should nag them till they release it into your area if they
don't have it there already!)
MIDDLE SHELF Coruba Pineapple Rum ($15–$16 for 750ml / Not available in the UK)
Cruzan Pineapple Rum ($12–$13 for 750ml / Not available in the UK)
Rum Jumbie Pineapple (Not available in the US £17 for 70cl or £23 for 1L)
BOTTOM SHELF Malibu Pineapple Rum ($13–$18 for 750ml / Not available in the UK)

SMOKED RUM
STOLEN Smoked Rum ($25 for 750 ml / Not Available in the UK)

From Sweet to Dry

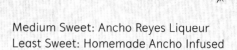

AN ADJUSTING GUIDE FOR DRINKING PALATES

When someone first approaches me for a drink and doesn't have a strong opinion of what they want, I try to guide them toward something suited for their palate even if they don't know what that is. I ask if they would like strong or weak, spicy or fruity, dry or sweet, and if they have any favourite flavours, they would like included. Often I am told by people that they like a drink, but it is too sweet or dry for their taste. One way to adjust sweetness is to withhold sugary syrups or ingredients in favour of equally flavourful but less sugary spirits or ingredients. To help with this, here is an example of an adjustment guide (by no means complete) to make drinks sweeter or drier depending on preference.

If swapping out similarly flavoured ingredients is not an option to adjust the sweetness, there are three other go-to tricks to try. First, one can add or withhold citrus (usually the lime juice or lemon juice). Secondly, one can add a float of a stronger spirit to make the drink dryer and more spirit-forward or cut the main spirit back to make the sweeter ingredients more pronounced. Thirdly, one can add soda water or more crushed ice to help dilute the recipe, or hold back on these ingredients to adjust the strength of the recipe. Remember that many drinks are meant to adjust over time as the crushed ice dissolves or spirit floats sink to the bottom of the glass. So, your impression of a drink may change as you drink. Even letting it rest will change the taste as the ice melts.

ALLSPICE/PIMENTO FLAVOURINGS
Very Sweet: Homemade Pimento Syrup
Sweet: Berry Hill Liqueur
Sweet: St. Elizabeth's Allspice Dram
Medium Sweet: Ed Hamilton's Pimento Dram

ANCHO FLAVOURINGS
Very Very Sweet: Homemade Ancho Chili Syrup
   (5-week shelf life when refrigerated)

Medium Sweet: Ancho Reyes Liqueur
Least Sweet: Homemade Ancho Infused
   Vodka or White Rum

BLOOD ORANGE FLAVOURINGS
Very Very Sweet: Monin Blood Orange Syrup
Medium Sweet: Solerno Blood Orange
   Liqueur
Sweet: San Pellegrino Blood Orange Soda
Least Sweet: Freshly Squeezed Blood Orange Juice

COCONUT FLAVOURINGS
Very Very Sweet: Coconut Syrup
Very Very Sweet: Cream of Coconut
Sweet: Coconut Rum
Least Sweet: Coconut Water

FALERNUM FLAVOURINGS
Very Very Sweet: Monin Falernum Syrup
Very Very Sweet: BG Reynolds Falernum Syrup
Very Very Sweet: Fee Brothers Falernum Syrup
Very Sweet: D. Taylor's Velvet Falernum Liqueur

GINGER FLAVOURINGS
Very Very Sweet: Ginger Syrup
Very Sweet: Ginger Reàl Squeeze
Sweet: Ginger Ale (weaker flavour) such as Vernor's
Sweet: Ginger Beer (stronger flavour) such as
   Cock 'n Bull, Fentimans or Fever Tree
Sweet: Domaine de Canton Ginger Liqueur

LEMON FLAVOURINGS
Very Very Sweet: Lemon Syrup
Sweet: Limoncello Lemon Liqueur
Least Sweet: Freshly Squeezed Lemon Juice

LIME FLAVOURINGS
Very Very Sweet: Rose's Lime Juice Cordial
Least Sweet: Freshly Squeezed Lime Juice

MINT FLAVOURINGS

Very Very Sweet: Mint Syrup
Very Sweet: Crème de Menthe Mint Liqueur
Least Sweet: Lightly Slapped Fresh Mint Leaves
    and/or Muddled

ORANGE FLAVOURINGS

Very Very Sweet: Monin Orange Syrup
Very Sweet: Hiram Walker Triple Sec
Very Sweet: BOLS Triple Sec
Medium Sweet: Cointreau
Medium Sweet: Senor's Orange Curaçao
Sweet: Freshly Squeezed Orange Juice
Dry: Grand Marnier
Very Dry: Pierre Ferrand Dry Curaçao Triple Sec

PEANUT FLAVOURINGS

Very Very Sweet: Peanut Orgeat Syrup
Very Sweet: Castries Peanut Liqueur
Least Sweet: Peanut Butter (some brands are
    sweeter than others)

PINEAPPLE FLAVOURINGS

Very Very Sweet: Pineapple Syrup
Very Sweet: Sweetened Pineapple Juice
Sweet: Fresh Unsweetened Pineapple Juice

Spirits

ABSINTHE: A once illegal anise (black liquorice) flavoured spirit with an infusion of wormwood, considered by some to be hallucinogenic and dangerous. The wormwood derivatives are now considered relatively innocuous. Absinthe has made a comeback in the US and elsewhere with its ingredients declared safe for consumption.

ALLSPICE LIQUEUR: See Pimento Dram. A liqueur made from allspice pimento berries that originated in Jamaica and is used in small proportions to add a flavourful spice.

AMARETTO: Almond flavoured liqueur. Modern amaretto is not always made entirely from almonds, but from the pits of peaches or, most often, apricots.

ANCHO REYES: Based on a 1927 recipe, Ancho Reyes is an authentic spicy liqueur crafted from ancho and poblano chiles in Puebla, Mexico.

ANGOSTURA BITTERS: Aromatic bitters originating in Angostura, Venezuela; now produced in Trinidad.

APEROL: An Italian aperitif, produced by the Campari company. Lower alcohol content than original Campari and milder in taste.

AQUAVIT: A flavoured spirit popular in Scandinavia that obtains its distinct taste from spices and herbs, especially caraway, dill, or anise.

BÉNÉDICTINE: A flavoured liqueur that uses 27 different herbs and spices. It's made by Benedictine monks from a secret recipe dating back to 1510.

BITTERS: A non-alcoholic aromatic combination of herbs, fruits, roots, barks, seeds, and flowers steeped in an alcohol base and then aged (see Angostura Bitters and Peychaud Bitters).

BLUE CURAÇAO: Blue coloured Dutch West Indian Curaçao orange liqueur. Produced in Holland.

BOURBON WHISKEY: American whiskey made by using at least 51% corn, with the remainder being rye, wheat, malted barley, singly or in any combination.

BRANDY: A product of the distillation of wine, or fruit in the case of flavoured brandies such as peach or cherry. Cognac and Armagnac are special varieties made from grapes grown in specific areas of France.

CACHAÇA: A Brazilian sugarcane-based spirit similar to rum but quite distinct. This is considered an inexpensive "working man's" spirit in South America and the quality ranges wildly. Our favourites are pot stilled and then barrel-aged in bourbon barrels or exotic South American hardwoods. They pick up some amazing flavours as they age. Some of the mass-produced unaged light/silver varieties can taste like jet fuel, so be careful what you use!

DOMAINE DE CANTON GINGER LIQUEUR: A liqueur that is 28 per cent alcohol (56 proof), is golden in colour, and is packaged in a bamboo-shaped bottle. It contains syrup made from crystallised Chinese baby ginger, Grand Champagne cognac, neutral spirit, orange blossom honey from Provence, and vanilla.

CHAMBORD: A French liqueur made from red and black raspberries, Madagascar vanilla, Moroccan citrus peel, honey and cognac.

CHARTREUSE: Yellow and green herbal liqueurs made only by the Carthusian monks of La Grande Chartreuse, France. Produced since 1605 from a secret recipe consisting of over 100 alpine herbs.

COFFEE LIQUEUR: A coffee flavoured liqueur. Kahlúa from Mexico is one of the most popular.

COGNAC: A type of brandy that has been distilled from wine made from grapes grown in the area surrounding the cities of Cognac and Jarnac.

COINTREAU: A French made, bitter-sweet orange flavoured liqueur. Produced by the Cointreau family since 1849. As well as a component of several well-known cocktails it is drunk as an apéritif and digestif.

CRÈME LIQUEUR: is a liqueur that has a great deal of additional sugar added to the point that it has a near-syrup consistency. Unlike cream liqueurs, crème liqueurs include no cream in their ingredients. "Crème" in this case refers to the consistency. Common flavours include blackcurrant, blackberry, chocolate and mint.

CRÈME DE BANANA: Banana flavoured liqueur.

CRÈME DE CACAO: A white or brown coloured liqueur made from cocoa beans, vanilla and spices.

CRÈME DE CASSIS: A French liqueur made from black currants.

CRÈME DE MENTHE: A red, green, or white coloured, peppermint flavoured liqueur.

CRÈME DE FRAMBOISE: A raspberry-flavoured liqueur.

CRÈME DE VIOLETTE: Violet-flavoured liqueur.

CURAÇAO: Orange-flavoured liqueur, produced mainly in France and the Netherlands, but originating from the Caribbean; made from the peels of oranges grown on the island of Curaçao, in the West Indies.

DRAMBUIE: A Scotch-based, honey flavoured liqueur, from Skye, that first appeared around the time of the Battle of Culloden in 1745. It was trademarked in 1893 and produced in Edinburgh since 1909.

DRY VERMOUTH: A French made, herb flavoured wine that is used in making drinks such as the Martini, the Manhattan and the Negroni. It was traditionally used for medicinal purpose.

FALERNUM: (pronounced fah-learn-um) is a sweet liqueur (or syrup) used in Caribbean and tropical drinks. It contains flavours of almond, ginger, cloves, and lime, and sometimes vanilla or allspice.

FRANGELICO: An Italian liqueur made with wild hazelnuts, berries and flowers.

GALLIANO: A yellow herb and spice liqueur made in Solaro, Italy. Named after an Italian hero.

GENEVER: A predecessor to the style of gin that we know today as London Dry Gin. Traditionally the base of Genever had a high percentage of Malt Wine (15%-50%), creating a spirit that had similar weight on the palate and malty notes like whiskey, and a herbal component that is common with gin.

GIN: A neutral alcohol base flavoured with juniper.

GRAND MARNIER: A cognac brandy-based liqueur flavoured with orange.

KAHLÚA: A coffee flavoured liqueur made in Mexico.

LILLET: A French wine-based aperitif from Podensac. Comes in varieties such as rouge, blanc and rosé.

LIMONCELLO: A distinctive, premium liqueur made with the juice of fresh lemons from Southern Italy.

LIQUEUR: Distilled spirit flavoured with such things as fruit, herbs, coffee, nuts, mint and chocolate.

LONDON GIN: The driest gin available.

MACADAMIA NUT LIQUEUR: Hawaiian macadamia nut flavoured liqueur. 26½% alcohol by volume (53 proof). Trader Vic's issues a popular variety.

MARASCHINO: Italian, cherry-flavoured liqueur — usually colourless, but may be red.

MELON LIQUEUR: Spirit-based, melon-flavoured liqueur, (See Midori).

MEZCAL: Similar to tequila but, unlike tequila which is typically made in one region from blue agave, mezcal can be made anywhere and can use one or more of up to 30 different types of agave. Mezcal is typically harsher and smokier flavoured than tequila thanks to roasting the agaves underground rather than cooking them in an oven. As with tequilas, mezcals are typically produced in blanco, reposado, or anejo varieties.

MIDORI: A sweet, bright green-coloured, muskmelon-flavoured liqueur. Its name is Japanese for "green".

NOCELLO: A a walnut flavoured liqueur from the Emilia-Romagna region of Italy.

PAMA LIQUEUR: A pomegranate liqueur. Other companies have produced pomegranate spirits, including a schnapps by Hiram Walker, but PAMA has a superb flavour.

PERNOD: Pernod Anise and Ricard Pastis, are both anise-flavoured liqueurs (black liquorice) and are often referred to as Pernod or Ricard. After the banning of absinthe, Pernod Ricard was created from the Pernod Fils company, which had produced absinthe. Despite the repeal of the absinthe ban, Pernod continues to be quite popular.

PETER HEERING CHERRY LIQUEUR: A world-renowned cherry flavoured liqueur. Produced since 1818 in Copenhagen, Denmark.

PEYCHAUD BITTERS: Created in 1830 by Antoine Peychaud in Haiti, now produced in New Orleans by the Sazerac Company.

PIMENTO DRAM: a spicy liqueur flavoured with allspice berries. It is also known as pimento dram because allspice is a berry from the Pimenta dioica tree. Originating in Jamaica and used in small proportions to add a flavourful spice. Berry Hill from Jamaica is hard to obtain in the US. St Elizabeth Allspice Dram is more commonly available. Recently, Ed Hamilton released a version that utilises pot still rum and has a funkier and spicier flavour, probably more in keeping with older/authentic recipes.

PISCO: A colourless or yellowish-to-amber coloured brandy produced in the winemaking regions of Peru and Chile. Made by distilling fermented grape juice into a high-proof spirit, it was developed by 16th-century Spanish settlers.

PORT: A red fortified dessert wine produced in Portugal.

RUM: Spirit made from the fermentation and distillation of sugar cane. Light, medium, and heavy bodied flavour variations exist as do variations in colour when not clear. Often flavoured with spices or fruit flavours. There is a huge swathe of rums, and they could be discussed at length in terms of geography, still type used, blending, or ageing methods. Typically, recipes up till now refer to the following general categories, although more exacting definitions are beginning to be used:

- **Overproof Rum:** Most rums sold in the United States are bottled at 80 to 100 proof, or 40 to 50 per cent alcohol by volume. Some exceptions are rums bottled at 125 to 160 proof or more. These rums tend to be more popular in the Caribbean Islands where locals prefer a stronger drink. They're also used in cooking recipes that call for rum to be ignited in flame (flambé) or drinks that blend a very strong rum into their recipe.

- **Demerara Rum:** A type of rum made in Guyana, on the northern coast of South America.

- **Blackstrap Molasses Rum:** A dark rum (one of the darkest) that is heavily flavoured with molasses. For the recipes in this book, we are referring to the Cruzan brand.

- **Navy Rum:** Navy rums are often a blend of dark rums, traditionally from English colonies such as Guyana, Trinidad, Jamaica, Bermuda and Barbados. Historically the alcohol content was greater than 57 per cent.

- **Dark Rum:** Many cocktail recipes call for dark, full-flavoured rums. Usually dark brown or reddish-brown in colour, these rich flavourful rums are frequently matured in barrels longer than gold rums but may just contain caramel colouring.

- **Gold Rum:** Rum mellows in barrels overtime, it takes on amber or golden hues. These golden rums usually present a more flavourful profile than the white or clear rums. They are often aged several years or more. But color is not always a reliable indicator of age.

- **Martinique Amber Rum:** Rhum agricole that has been aged in wood casks to achieve an amber hue and richer flavour than the younger agricole rum.

- **Martinique Rhum Agricole Blanc:** The Appellation d'Origine Contrôlée for Martinique rhum agricole is a standard of production, ageing and labelling. Rhum Agricole is also produced in Guadeloupe and Mauritius. Often described as having a "grassy" aftertaste.

- **White or Light Rum:** Ideal for mixing in cocktails, white, silver, clear or crystal rums are generally without strong flavours. They're often aged for a minimal amount of time and filtered to remove most, if not all colour.

- **Spiced Rum:** There is a wide range of spiced rum, but it usually consists of gold or dark rum infused with a spice or flavouring blend, such as vanilla, cinnamon, anise, cloves, allspice, or orange.

- **Flavoured or Infused Rum:** This usually consists of white rum that is infused or flavoured with a specific flavour (such as coconut, vanilla, orange, or pineapple).

RYE WHISKEY: American whiskey must be made from a mash containing at least 51 per cent rye. Canadian whiskey does not have to contain any rye at all to label itself "rye" as that is considered in Canada to be a historical term.

SAMBUCA: Italian, anise flavoured liqueur often served flaming with coffee beans.

SCHNAPPS: American schnapps is an alcoholic beverage that is produced by mixing neutral grain spirit with fruit or other flavours.

SCOTCH WHISKY: A malt whisky or grain whisky made in Scotland and aged in oak barrels for at least three years.

SLOE GIN: A red liqueur made by steeping sloe berries in gin — previously homemade but now commercially available.

ST. GERMAIN: A liqueur created in the artisanal French manner from freshly hand-picked elderflower blossoms.

SWEET VERMOUTH: An Italian made, herb flavoured wine. Used in making drinks such as Rob Roys and Manhattans.

TUACA: A brand of liqueur originally produced by the Tuoni and Canepa families of Livorno, Italy, and now produced by Brown-Forman of Louisville, Kentucky. It has a vanilla and citrus flavour.

TEQUILA: Mexican spirit distilled from the blue agave plant. Tequila can only be made in the state of Jalisco. Generally available in three categories: Blanco (unaged), Reposado (rested) and Anejo (aged).

TRIPLE SEC: A strong, sweet, colourless, orange-flavoured liqueur.

VERMOUTH: Wine-based aperitif flavoured with extracts of wormwood — both sweet and dry vermouths are widely used in cocktails.

VODKA: Colourless, grain-based spirit, originally from Russia and Poland. Now made from virtually any grain, many fruits and potatoes as well and available in dozens of flavours.

WHISKEY: Spirit distilled from grain in either Ireland or North America. Corn, rye and barley are all used.

WHISKY: A spirit from Scotland traditionally distilled from grain in the lowlands and barley in the rest of the country. Also known as Scotch Whisky.

Ingredients

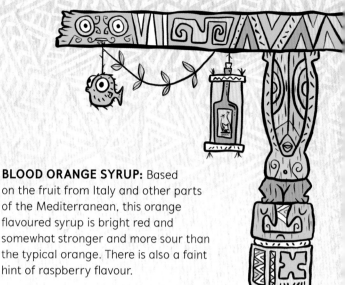

AGAVE SYRUP (HONEY OR NECTAR)**:** Agave syrup is a sweetener commercially produced from several species of agave. It is sweeter than honey and tends to be less viscous. Most agave syrup comes from Mexico and South Africa. It comes in both lighter and darker grades, but for these recipes, we prefer medium dark.

ANCHO CHILLI SYRUP: This is a syrup made with ancho chiles. The ancho chilli is the dried version of the poblano pepper. Ancho chiles have a deep red colour and a wrinkled skin. Anchos are sweet and smoky with a flavour slightly reminiscent of raisins. Their heat is mild to medium-hot. See our receipe on page 238.

APPLE CIDER: The name used in the United States and parts of Canada for an unfiltered, unsweetened, non-alcoholic beverage made from apples. Though typically referred to simply as "cider" in those areas, it is not to be confused with the alcoholic beverage known as cider throughout most of Europe, called hard cider in North America. It is typically opaque due to fine apple particles in suspension and generally tangier than conventionally filtered apple juice, depending on the apples used. Today, most commercial cider is treated to kill bacteria and extend its shelf life, but untreated cider can still be found. For the purposes of these recipes, we used unpasteurized and unfiltered cider available from local orchards for the freshest and most intense flavour.

APRICOT NECTAR: Apricots are small orange-coloured fruits related to peaches and plums. Nectar is a heavier consistency than juice.

BASIL LEAF: This is an aromatic annual herb of the mint family, native to tropical Asia. The leaves of the basil plant are used as a culinary herb, especially in Mediterranean dishes.

BLOOD ORANGE SYRUP: Based on the fruit from Italy and other parts of the Mediterranean, this orange flavoured syrup is bright red and somewhat stronger and more sour than the typical orange. There is also a faint hint of raspberry flavour.

BROWN SUGAR: Either an unrefined or partially refined soft sugar consisting of sugar crystals with some residual molasses content (natural brown sugar), or it is produced by the addition of molasses to refined white sugar (commercial brown sugar).

CALAMANSI LIME JUICE: Calamansi is a variety of lime used in Southeast Asia cuisines, especially in Malaysia, Singapore, Indonesia, and the Philippines. It can be best described as a sort of hybrid between orange and lime. They have an orange pulp, but the juice is sour and tart. For the purposes of these recipes, we use cartoned juice provided by Sun Tropics.

CARAMEL SYRUP: This can add a sweet buttery flavour to a cocktail. Much of the complexity comes from the burn of the sugars. Think of how they torch a crème brûlée. Some people even make their own "burned sugar" syrup. They play with different kinds of sugars and rates of burn until they find their favourite. Careful, though, these burned flavours can easily overwhelm a cocktail.

CHAMOMILE SYRUP: Chamomile has a bittersweet flowery taste and is most often associated with herbal teas, but in small amounts it can be delicious. You can make this yourself. See our recipe on page 238.

CHERRIES: Tom has a preference for Tillen Farms jarred cherries, especially the Bada Bing cherries. Kelly likes the maraschino cherries by Luxardo. You can also make your own cocktail cherries. Whatever you do, though, don't use the generic red food dyed maraschino cherries!

CHERRY JUICE: There are several very good choices for fresh pressed and refrigerated bottled juices these days. Don't buy cherry juice that's been cut with apple or other juices. Get the good stuff.

CHERRY SYRUP: Monin brand is usually our go-to, but sometimes we'll use the jarred juice from some of our premium cherries. Always leave just enough juice to cover the fruit that's left. Don't ever throw the juice away! Waste not, want not.

CHINESE FIVE SPICE SYRUP: This is a syrup including star anise, cloves, Chinese cinnamon, Sichuan pepper, and fennel seeds. Some recipes may contain anise seed, ginger, nutmeg, turmeric, or cardamom. For our recipe see page 238.

CILANTRO (CORIANDER)**:** The bright, spicy flavour of cilantro has long served as a flavour enhancer. A wild herb that dates from the Neolithic era, the leaves and seeds of cilantro have been used to make perfume in Ancient Greece, rye bread in Russia, beer in Belgium and sausages in South Africa. Known in most of the world as coriander, this pungent herb is used in the cuisines of Asia, Africa, India and the Mediterranean. Spanish explorers, who called the plant cilantro, brought it to the New World where it became popular in Mexican cooking. It is especially good in tequila-based drinks.

CINNAMON POWDER: Not only is this delicious, but it can also be used for a pyrotechnic display by sprinkling it over some already flaming overproof rum in a spent lime shell. Be careful. There are lots of things in a tiki hut that catch fire easily!

CINNAMON SYRUP: Tom prefers BG Reynolds brand which is a bit on the strong side. Kelly usually makes her own homemade version. If you make your own, there are different cinnamon sticks from different regions, but we favour the Indonesian or Saigon/Vietnamese with its higher oil content (tastes like red hot candies). In a pinch, however, you can always use Torani or Monin brands.

COCA-COLA: A popular brand of cola with a dark caramel colour and flavoured with vanilla and cinnamon with trace amounts of orange, lime and lemon. We tend to use the Mexican variant which comes in glass bottles and contains sugar cane rather than high-fructose corn syrup.

COCO LÓPEZ: A mixture of sugarcane syrup and coconut cream. Coco López was the base for the invention of the tropical drink, piña colada. Ordinarily sold in a can, this mixture is widely regarded as a better product than newer, cheaper mixtures, which often use chemicals and preservatives. Many of the recipes in this book call for Coco Reàl, which is an acceptable substitute, but use Coco López if you can.

COCONUT CREAM: See Coco López above and Reàl Coconut Squeeze.

COCOPANDAN SYRUP: Cocopandan syrup is a common product in Southeast Asian cuisines and beverages. It is made from coconut syrup and pandan juice. The pandan element lends a grassy fragrance and a flavour not unlike basmati rice. In most cases, the syrup is sold with green or red food colouring added, but in its pure state it is colourless. For the purposes of these recipes, we use Marjan Boudoin brand bottled syrup from Indonesia which has some red food colouring and is marketed as a syrup flavouring for shave ice. Available at many Asian markets.

COFFEE: With the rise of coffee houses and the ubiquitous nature of a Starbucks on every street corner, coffee may not seem that exotic to many people. However, it has long been a staple ingredient in some of the most celebrated tiki cocktails, including the Black Magic at the Mai-Kai restaurant in Florida. Most drinks call for a dark roast coffee, usually a Kona Blend. However, you can play with other dark roasts if you like, including Jamaican or Italian Espresso.

CUCUMBER SPEAR: Suggested garnish for the Bokor's Bastard. Cucumber gives a clean, crisp note.

CRACKED BLACK PEPPER SYRUP: Be sure to use freshly cracked whole peppercorns for this homemade syrup. This stuff is delicious. Kelly's recipe is on page 239. Tom's simple version is on page 238.

CREAM (HEAVY WHIPPING)**:** This ingredient is as essential for the dairy flavour as it is for the heavier consistency and "mouth feel" it provides. We don't use it in many cocktails, and it can turn rancid quickly in the fridge, so keep an eye on the expiration date.

CRUSHED ICE: We've used many varieties of ice over the years. Refrigerators with built-in ice crushers in the door are rather handy. You can also buy stand-alone electric crushers, use the old-fashioned hand-crank ice crushers which are easy to find at vintage stores and thrift shops or smash your own with a mallet. Ice is very important, and many drinks have a strategy so that layers or floats will permeate through the crushed ice overtime to regulate your drink. The rate of melt does influence the flavour. Just make sure your ice is fresh. Nothing worse than ruining a drink with ice that has absorbed bad refrigerator flavours.

DATE PUREE: Kelly's drink, The Alexander, uses a date puree. See the recipe on page 242 to make your own. Tom advises you to take any un-pureed dates and stuff them with almonds and goat cheese, then wrap them in bacon and throw them in the oven as a fantastic cocktail appetiser!

FIVE-PEPPER SYRUP: Kelly uses this in her Cocktail Corrido, and made a small batch using Kozlowski brand Five Pepper Preserves from our local Pavillion's store. Very flavourful. Made of half preserves and half water, heated to form a syrup or simply use your lemon or lime juice citrus component to dissolve the preserves before adding to a shaker.

GINGER BEER: This is a non-alcoholic but more intense version of ginger ale used in many cocktails (like a Dark 'n' Stormy). There are several good versions out on the market. Be careful, because some have additional fruit flavours added and you don't want to add unexpected flavours to a recipe. We usually use Cock 'n Bull or Gosling's brand. For a stronger flavour, Fever-Tree is also a good choice.

GINGER SYRUP: There are many commercial varieties to choose from. BG Reynold's makes a good version. You can also make your own at home. Our recipe is on page 240.

GRAPEFRUIT JUICE: Always use white grapefruit juice, not pink or ruby red. Fresh pressed juice is preferred, but as it is seasonal, it's not always available. You can get, however, bottled white grapefruit juice from Ocean Spray if you are in a pinch. It's not ideal, but it will work.

GRENADINE: A pomegranate syrup used in a variety of drinks such as the Singapore Sling or the Shirley Temple. Try to avoid the older and more common Rose's brand because of its use of high fructose corn syrup and because it just isn't very good. There are many newer brands on the market with good flavour that use cane syrup. BG Reynold's Hibiscus Grenadine is tasty. It's also easy to make your own.

GUANABANA JUICE (SEE SOURSOP JUICE)**:** This spiky fruit grows in parts of Latin America, the Caribbean, Africa, Southeast Asia and the Pacific. The flavour of Guanabana has been described as a combination of strawberry and pineapple, with sour citrus flavour notes contrasting with an underlying creamy flavour reminiscent of coconut or banana. For the purposes of these recipes, we use cartoned juice provided by Sun Tropics.

GUAVA NECTAR: This comes from a pale orange tropical fruit with pink, juicy flesh and a strong, sweet aroma. Nectar is a heavier consistency of juice.

HIBISCUS SYRUP: Made with dried "Jamaica" (Hibiscus) flowers. This flavour has been used for years to make a non-alcoholic drink (often seen at Mexican street vendors' booths alongside Horchata and Agua de Tamarindo). You can purchase dried flowers in the Mexican spice section of your local supermarket and make a homemade version yourself. See our recipe on page 240.

HONEY SYRUP: A syrup made of equal parts honey and water. Always use the finest clover honey available. Honey was a major part of many classic tiki cocktails (especially at Don the Beachcomber's) and imparts flavour as well as a heavier "mouth-feel."

LAVENDER SYRUP: Monin makes a very good lavender syrup. You can, of course, make your own as well, using fresh lavender and a simple syrup base. You can see our recipe on page 240.

LEMONGRASS SYRUP: This lends a grassy/citrusy flavour to cocktails. These days you can purchase lemongrass in most supermarkets and make a home-made version yourself. See our recipe on page 240.

LEMON JUICE: When we say lemons, unless otherwise indicated, we mean regular lemons, not Meyer lemons. Fresh juice is always preferred, and if you are making just a few cocktails, a hand squeezer should be good enough. For large batches, however, you might want to consider using an industrial lever juice press.

LEMON WEDGE: Wedges and decorative strips of lemon peel contain oil which can add another dimension of flavour beyond just the juice; they are often more than just decorative.

LIME JUICE: Fresh juice is always preferred, and if you are making just a few cocktails, a green hand squeezer should be good enough. However, for large batches, you might want to consider using an industrial lever juice press.

LIME WEDGE: Wedges, lime halves, and decorative strips of peel contain lime oil which can add another dimension of flavour beyond just the juice; again, they are often more than just decorative.

MANGO NECTAR: This comes from a green and orange-skinned tropical fruit with bright orange flesh and a large oblong pit, sometimes called a stone. For the recipes in this book, we used Kern's Farm mango nectar. Nectar is a heavier consistency of juice.

MINT SPRIG: A standard garnish for many tiki cocktails. If you buy them from the grocer, wrap them in a damp paper towel and refrigerate them so they keep for longer. You can grow your own, but you might want to keep them in a separate pot because they will flourish like Kudzu vine!

ORANGE JUICE: Freshly Squeezed juice is always preferable, but be careful because the taste can vary wildly. Processed commercial juices have taken uniformity to an art form, so you know what the taste will be each time.

ORANGE WEDGE: Try to use the freshest and ripest oranges you can find. Remove the seeeds and bits of pith with a bar knife before garnishing.

ORGEAT ALMOND SYRUP: This is one of the most essential ingredients on every tiki bar. It is used to make the classic Mai Tai as well as other drinks. Trader Vic's brand used to be a go-to, but it has fallen out of favour because of its use of artificial ingredients. We prefer to make our own. There are several good recipes online and in books. If you must use a commercial make, we recommend BG Reynolds brand, or if you have no other higher end alternative, use Torani.

PASSIONFRUIT SYRUP: Next to orgeat syrup, this is one of the most important tropical cocktail syrups. Many of our recipes list Torani because that's what we had available at the time. Changing out the Torani on our recipes is going to change the taste profile, and Kelly doesn't advise it. For those cocktails that don't specify Torani Passionfruit, we suggest making your own or using a craft cocktail-friendly commercial syrup such as those by BG Reynolds or Small Hand Foods. If you have no other craft version, use Torani.

PEACH NECTAR: Made from the classic round sweet fruit with white or yellow flesh. For the recipes in this book, we use Kern's Farm peach nectar. Nectar is a heavier consistency of juice.

PEANUT ORGEAT SYRUP: Like orgeat almond syrup, but made with peanuts. See our recipe on page 240. Used in Trader Tom's Peanut Mug Salute! on page 240.

PINEAPPLE (CRUSHED): Fresh is best. We suggest investing in a pineapple ring corer and then you can even serve drinks in your hollowed-out pineapples. At a pinch you can use canned.

PINEAPPLE JUICE: Again, fresh is best, and there is something about the flavour and acidity from a ripe and freshly cored pineapple that is hard to beat. However, we frequently use mini cans of Dole Pineapple juice. For a few drinks here and there it makes more sense than opening a big container and having the leftovers go bad in the fridge once the party is over.

PISTACHIO SYRUP: This syrup was commercially produced by Monin for a time (and may still be), but we've had a hard time locating some recently. You can, however, always make your own. To try, see our recipe on page 240.

POMEGRANATE SYRUP: See Grenadine.

PRICKLY PEAR CACTUS SYRUP: Most commonly associated with margaritas and other tequila-based cocktails. Prickly pears, when prepared correctly, can have a delicious flavour (something like strawberry and bubble-gum). There are many commercial varieties of prickly pear syrup available. If you wish to try making your own see our recipe on page 241.

PUMPKIN SPICE (OR PUMPKIN PIE) SYRUP: For the drinks listed here, we like to use the Torani brand but other brands are available.

REÀL COCONUT SQUEEZE: Comparable to Coco López as a coconut cream. We would agree that Coco López has a better flavour, but this product comes in a handy squeeze bottle, doesn't separate and congeal as easily, and requires no refrigeration after opening. They have an extensive line of different flavoured squeeze products, but the only two we've tried have been the original coconut and the ginger. You may substitute Coco López for this if you prefer.

REÀL GINGER SQUEEZE: Similar to the Coconut Squeeze, the Ginger Squeeze has a thick syrupy consistency and more "body" than a straight syrup. A solid product that, again, is easy to dispense and requires no refrigeration after opening.

RHUBARB SYRUP: Rhubarb comes in long celery-like stalks but make sure you get red ones and not the unripe green ones if you are making this syrup

yourself. Rhubarb has a great flavour and makes wonderful syrup. To try, see our recipe on page 241.

ROCK CANDY SYRUP: A sweeter, thicker version of simple syrup. It's made from 2 parts sugar, 1 part water, brought to a boil, lowered to a simmer and simmered for 5 minutes, then removed from the heat and allowed to cool.

ROSEBUD SYRUP: Rosebud syrup is a simple syrup that's infused with rose petals. It can add a mild floral taste and light pink hue to a drink, depending on how much you use. For these recipes, we use Marjan Boudoin brand bottled syrup from Indonesia which has some food colouring and citrus flavouring enhancers and is marketed as a syrup flavouring for shave ice. Available in many Asian supermarkets.

SESAME SEED/OIL SYRUP: Used in Tom's Tahitian Twister cocktail, this syrup is easy to make. See our recipe on page 241.

SIMPLE SYRUP: A syrup made from 1 part sugar and 1 part water, brought to a boil, lowered to a simmer and simmered for 5 minutes, then removed from the heat and allowed to cool.

SODA WATER: This is not to be confused with tonic water which includes quinine. If you desire tonic, we recommend the Fever-Tree brand. For carbonated water, we suggest buying small bottles of Schweppes seltzer or another leading brand. Soda water differs from seltzer slightly in that it often contains a small amount of sodium. Small bottles are manageable and less wasteful. If you buy a large 2 litre of carbonated soda water, you aren't likely to use the entire bottle before it goes flat. For a touch of class you can use a soda water dispenser with CO2 cartridges. It's great for Marx Brother routines as well.

SOURSOP JUICE (SEE GUANABANA JUICE): This spiky fruit grows in parts of Latin America, the Caribbean, Africa, Southeast Asia and the Pacific. The flavour of Soursop has been described as a combination of strawberry and pineapple, with sour citrus flavour notes contrasting with an underlying creamy flavour reminiscent of coconut or banana. You can buy it in a carton at most large supermarkets.

SWEET AND SOUR MIX: The commercial brands of sweet and sour mix are basically what killed the idea of tropical cocktails during the 1980s when tiki fell out of fashion. Commercial mixes tend to taste artificial and have a slew of chemicals added. If you wish to make your own add freshly squeezed lemon and lime juice to a simple syrup.

TAMARIND SYRUP: The tamarind tree produces pod-like fruit which is a legume (like peanuts). Many in California and the Southwest are familiar with *agua de tamarindo*, which is a traditional Mexican beverage made from tamarind syrup and water, served cold.

Tamarind is sweet, tart, and has a variety of culinary uses, ranging from desserts to Worcestershire sauce. We have used it in a couple of cocktails, including Tom's Aztec Hotel. If you want to make your own tamarind syrup head to page 242 for a recipe.

WATERMELON JUICE: Cold pressed containers can be purchased at Whole Foods and other retailers. Or, you can press your own. Delicious! The sediment tends to settle and must be shaken before used.

WATERMELON SYRUP: For the drinks listed here, we use the Monin or Torani brands.

Drinks by Strength

Note that this is not by total volume or by proof of alcohol. This is simply by the total number of oz of alcoholic spirits consumed within each serving size portion of drink. So, it is a rough approximation.

NON ALCOHOLIC: 1 SHRUNKEN HEAD
0 total oz

None... Sorry! Virgin drinks or Mocktails could be a whole other book.

WEAK: 2 SHRUNKEN HEADS
1-2¼ total oz

MODERATE: 3 SHRUNKEN HEADS
2.26-3½ total oz

STRONG: 4 SHRUNKEN HEADS
3.6-4½ total oz

VERY STRONG: 5 SHRUNKEN HEADS
4.6 or higher total oz

Drinks by Creator

CO-CREATED

Ingredients

Absinthe, 91, 144, 162, 233
Agave Syrup/Agave Honey/Agave Nectar, 182, 185, 111
Allspice Liqueur/Pimento Dram, 68, 75, 91, 111, 120, 132, 147, 151, 178
Amaretto, 72, 80, 188, 191
Ancho Chili Syrup, 71, 79, 83, 99, 100, 103, 119, 123, 127, 136, 185, 209, 229, 238
Ancho Reyes, 75, 95, 143, 177, 209
Aperol, 83, 152, 161, 210
Apple Cider, 95, 152, 209, 230
Apricot Nectar, 99
Aquavit, 80, 148

Bénédictine and Brandy/B&B, 199, 214
Bitters, 79, 83, 87, 95, 104, 108, 112, 128, 131, 136, 144, 148, 151, 161, 165, 170, 173, 178, 185, 191, 202, 214, 217, 221, 226, 233
Blackstrap Molasses Rum, 68, 72, 84, 92, 99, 147, 151
Blood Orange Syrup, 72, 112, 144, 148, 233, 234
Blue Curaçao, 72, 75, 132, 192, 214
Bourbon Whiskey, 170, 173, 174, 177, 178
Brandy, 72, 83, 134, 188, 196, 230

Cachaça, 182, 185
Calamansi Lime Juice, 155
Domaine de Canton Ginger Liqueur, 103, 108, 116, 123, 127, 131, 162, 170, 202, 218, 226, 229
Caramel Syrup, 72, 120
Chambord, 83, 107, 112, 136, 139, 166, 191
Chamomile Syrup, 108, 116, 238
Cherry Juice, 214
Cherry Syrup, 95, 115, 199, 234
Chinese Five Spice Syrup, 92, 107, 238
Cinnamon Syrup, 75, 104, 108, 111, 120, 132, 144, 177, 209, 226, 230, 233
Coca-Cola, 120
Coco López/Coconut Cream, 112
Coco Reàl Squeeze, 71, 72, 80, 83, 99, 107, 111, 112, 115, 119, 131, 132

Coconut Cream, 68, 71, 80, 107, 112, 115
Cocopandan Syrup, 155
Coffee, 120
Cognac, 152, 162, 191, 199, 209, 230
Cointreau, 76, 91, 95, 111, 140, 217
Cracked Black Pepper Syrup, 119, 123, 135, 155, 229, 238-239
Crème De Banana, 87
Crème De Cassis, 72, 84, 147
Curaçao, 88, 112, 123, 147, 170, 178, 206, 234

Dark Rum, 68, 72, 76, 83, 87, 88, 91, 99, 100, 107, 111, 112, 116, 120, 124, 132, 135, 136, 144, 148, 151, 152, 233, 234
Demerara Rum, 80, 88, 91, 103, 104, 108, 111, 119, 120, 123, 136, 143, 144, 148, 151, 155, 226, 229, 233, 234
Drambuie, 92, 173
Dry Vermouth, 214

Falernum, 76, 100, 107, 108, 166, 170, 221, 226, 234
Five-Pepper Syrup, 205
Frangelico, 119

Galliano, 75, 192, 199
Genever, 196, 230
Gin, 158, 161, 162, 165, 166, 170, 188, 191, 192, 199
Ginger Beer, 88, 104, 170, 182, 199, 202
Ginger Reàl Squeeze, 88
Ginger Syrup, 88, 124, 131, 136, 165, 182, 240
Grand Marnier, 80, 88, 107, 120, 127, 206, 229
Grapefruit Juice, 68, 103, 108, 120, 151, 158, 217
Grenadine/Pomegranate Syrup, 80, 104, 132, 148
Guanabana Juice/Soursop Juice, 155
Guava Nectar, 68, 80, 103, 107, 111, 112, 119, 127, 128, 131, 132, 144, 148, 152, 182, 185, 233, 234

Acknowledgements

We would like to thank Sven Kirsten, Bosko Hrnjak, Otto Von Stroheim, Danny & Stephanie Gallardo, Ben & Vicki Bassham, Al Evans, Ted Haigh, David Wondrich, Jeff Berry, Martin Cate, Michelle Trott, Tom D. Kline and Sherri Cliette, Jim Bacchi, Michael Hantula, Eric October and Manuel Nunez, Ernie Keen, Kevin Murphy and Claudia Murphy, Jeremy Fleener, David and Patricia Kilmer, Boris Hamilton, Jake Geiger, Kris Reifer, Jocelyn Sia, Adrian Eustaquio, Kevin & Valerie Upthegrove, Anders Anderson, David Eck, Tim & Teresa Harris, Rose Marston, Misha Body, Kimberly Noble, Mark Nolan, Bill Graff & Maria Ferro, Joseph Wythe, Holden Westland, John Okanishi, Kari Hendler, Rory Snyder, Dean Hess, Melanie Link, Beth Purcott, Marty Lush, Todd Meeker, and Peter Gick. And a shout-out to *The Desert Oasis Room Podcast, The 5 Minutes of Rum Podcast,* and the *This is Tiki!* Facebook group page. Thanks, also, to Hanford Lemoore and his website, *Tiki Central.* Lastly, a big thank you to our family members, who have suffered through our overwhelming obsession with all things tiki and who have been willing guinea pigs to a million failed cocktails that never made it into this present volume.

Credits

Interior text pen and ink illustrations by **TIKI TONY** · Chapter heading pen and ink illustrations by **JAKE GEIGER** · Additional art selections by **DOUG HORNE** · Photography editor/photography by **CASEY PROUT** · Additional drink photography by **MARK GROVER** · Additional drink photography by **MIKE HANTTULA** · Title type lettering by **IVAN CASTRO**.

Many thanks to **JIM BACCHI**, founder and composer of the Tikiyaki Orchestra, whose song titles were freely given to use as several of our cocktail names. See Aloha Baby (p. 68), Black Sand Blue Sea (p. 72), Exotique (p. 83), Pohō Moku (p. 127), Shaka Hula Bossa Nova (p. 136), Stranded In Paradise (p. 139), Bachelor Number One (p. 158), Singapore Swing (p. 199), Bachelor Number Two (p. 214), Dan-O's Day Off (p. 217), and the Pohō Moku Bowl (p. 229).

Home tiki bar photography by the following: Dawn Frasier's Bamboo Grove of Westwood by **SVEINN PHOTOGRAPHY**, Tiki tOny & Alene's The Beachcomber Shack by **CASEY PROUT**, Pete Klockau's & Katie Monachos's The Black Lagoon Room by **ALLOY PHOTOGRAPHY**, Matt Marble's The Breezeway by **CASEY PROUT**, Adrian Eustaquio's The Desert Oasis Room by **CASEY PROUT**, Jorge & Liz Romero's Frankie's Tiki Oasis by **CASEY PROUT**, Michael Uhlenkott & Alan Smart's HaleKahiki by **CASEY PROUT**, Ken & Gloria Hudson's Ken's Tiki Lounge by **CASEY PROUT**, Jeff Bannow's The Lili Kai Club by **JEFF BANNOW**, Caroline Roe & Robert Fertig's The Moai Icehouse by **CAROLINE ROE**, Mark Skipper's The Overlook Lounge by **HOLLY WEST PHOTOGRAPHY**, Ron & Mickee Ferrell's The Rincon Room by **CASEY PROUT**, Kirby & Polly Fleming's The Rumpus Room by **TOM D. KLINE**, Sven Kirsten's Silverlake Tiki Island by **TOM D. KLINE**, Erich Troudt's The Tiki Hut by **ERICH TROUDT**, Richard Barne's Trader Dick's by **RICHARD BARNES**, Kevin & Claudia Murphy's Waikiki Womb by **KATIE KLINE PHOTOGRAPHY**.

Tiki tOny hanging out in the lanai area of his Beachcomber Shack.

Kelly "HipHipaHula" Reilly

Kelly Reilly is a Los Angeles area mixologist and bartender who has spent years experimenting with the rich, complex and robust world of craft cocktails. With a mix of classic and original recipes, her focus is on bringing quality ingredients, amazing flavour and precise craft back to exotic, tropical and tiki cocktails. At the Tonga Hut in North Hollywood, she was instrumental in revamping their tiki cocktails menu and helped to organise their Loyal Order of the Drooling Bastard program. In addition to her event bartending, she sometimes serves as a host bartender at places like the speakeasy-themed La Descarga, in Los Angeles and both Tonga Hut locations.

"Trader" Tom Morgan

Tom lives in the West Hills of Southern California's San Fernando Valley. Many know him as the mysterious template maker for Humuhumu's tiki mug collection website, Ooga-Mooga.com. Tom also has a PhD specialising in nineteenth and twentieth-century American literature and film adaptation. He has taught college classes across Southern California with an emphasis on screenwriting, film, and public speaking. In his spare time and for over a decade Tom has been working to fill tiki mugs with the tastiest drinks possible at home bars, and tiki-themed events. When not writing or working, Tom can be found at home, sipping one of his latest concoctions and listening to Martin Denny on vinyl.